Shut Up

A journey into the lost art of listening

By Richard Dillon

Shut Up – A journey into the lost art of listening

Copyright © 2025 by Good Uke Publishing

All rights reserved. No part of this publication may be reproduced, distributed, or transmitted in any form or by any means, including photocopying, recording, or other electronic or mechanical methods, without the prior written permission of the publisher, except in the case of brief quotations used in critical reviews or scholarly articles.

Published by Good Uke Publishing

shutup@goodukepublishing.com

This is a work of creative nonfiction. Some names and identifying details have been changed to protect privacy. Conversations and scenes are based on true events, though dialogue and timelines may have been adjusted for clarity and narrative flow.

Ai was used in the cover image, research and editing of this book.

To Antoinette, Phoenix, and Xavier,

the best ukes I could ever ask for.

As Sensei keeps telling me,

"Teach what you need to learn."

Join the conversation online and be part of the Shut Up community.

Connect with others exploring the art of listening, share your reflections, and discover new content from Richard Dillon.

Follow and join us here:

YouTube
www.youtube.com/@shutupthebook

Instagram
www.instagram.com/shutupthebook

Facebook
www.facebook.com/shutupthebook/

TikTok
www.tiktok.com/@shutupthebook

Contents

Introduction	11
Part I: Noise	
Chapter 1. A call to listen	25
The noise we swim in	29
It started with a mop	33
The sound before the listening	36
Chapter 2. Why people don't need your opinion	39
Drowning in opinions	44
The psychological impact of unsolicited advice	47
The role of social media in amplifying opinions	50
Active, reflective & empathetic listening	53
Chapter 3. What gets in the way	57
Holding without fixing	60
The space between	63
Back to you	66
Chapter 4. The science of listening	71
The quiet power of presence	75
Learning to listen to what's not being said	83
Closing the distance	86

Part II: Practice

Chapter 5. The art of listening	93
Letting go of control	99
How we shape what we hear	105
The edge of listening	107
Chapter 6. Different ways of listening	111
Learning to listen with more than ears	114
Black belt listening	125
Is anyone there?	128
Chapter 7. Listening to your kids	133
Seeing eye to eye	136
Don't be so dramatic	139
A test	142
Chapter 8. Listening to your partner	145
Listening for the need	150
The cost of being right	153
Listening as a love language	157
Chapter 9. Listening at work	163
Seek first to understand	166
The spaces between roles	169
One call, everything changed	172

Contents

Part III: Deepening

Chapter 10. Back to the beginning	179
Sacred listening across traditions	185
How the world understood listening	188
The erosion of listening in modern culture	191
Chapter 11. How listening changes relationships	195
Why we harden	199
What lets us soften	201
A mountain to climb	203
Chapter 12. Listening to Yourself	209
Stillness as self-attunement	213
Plenty of time	219
The practice of staying	221
Afterword	225
References	229
Acknowledgement	235
About the author	237

Introduction

It was winter. I can't remember if it was raining, but the sky carried that heavy, unspoken promise. The clouds hung low, swollen and grey, as if the whole day was bracing to break. The air had that metallic stillness to it, the kind that makes everything feel suspended, as though the moment had paused mid-inhale.

We were in that café on the corner, the one with the uneven tables and chipped blue mugs. You know the one. It always carried the same scent, cardamom faintly threaded with something older, something that reminded me of the breath of worn books. Memory seemed to linger there, quiet and constant, just beneath the surface.

He sat across from me, and something in the way he held himself had changed. His body seemed folded in, not collapsed but drawn inward, as if retreating, trying to take up less space. His hands circled a mug he had not sipped from, the steam long since disappeared, while his eyes fixed on a point just over my shoulder, avoiding mine with a careful distance, as though eye contact might undo him.

He was coming out of a breakup, not the dramatic kind with slammed doors or sharp betrayals, but the kind that disintegrates quietly and still manages to hollow you out. I felt the absence of it more than I knew the details, a grief that arrives without spectacle, moves without warning, and settles in the chest like fog, stealing your voice before anyone even notices.

When he spoke it came in fragments, his mouth reaching for something his heart had not yet learned how to hold.

"I don't even know what happened," he said. "She told me she needed space. It feels like I'm watching my life from the outside."

There it was, the reflex you probably know yourself, the impulse to say something helpful, to patch over the rawness with borrowed comforts we have all collected over the years. My mind began scanning for the familiar phrases we keep close for moments like this.

Sometimes people come into our lives to teach us something. You're going to grow from this. She wasn't your soul partner. I even opened my mouth, but something in me stopped. It was quiet, and it was clear.

Shut Up.

So I did. I let my mouth close again and allowed the silence to rise between us, not as something awkward or heavy but as a presence in its own right. It held its ground without demand, offering space without

Introduction

expectation. It was a silence that allowed the moment to just be.

I stayed with him, not only in body but in the ache he had not yet translated, in the weight of what remained unnamed. There was no need to fill the space or shape the moment, because being there was already enough.

He kept staring into his coffee as if it might answer back, his thumb tracing the rim of the mug in slow, unconscious circles. Gradually, almost imperceptibly, something in him began to shift. His shoulders loosened, and his breath settled into a slower, more grounded rhythm. When his eyes finally met mine, they carried the sense of having just returned from somewhere far away.

We did not speak much after that. We simply sat together in the stillness and let the quiet be enough. Eventually, almost under his breath, he said, "Thanks for being here." Something in me shifted as well, not loud or sudden but more like a small alignment, something clicking quietly into place.

I don't think I had ever truly listened to someone before, not in that way, not without trying to shape their pain into something meaningful or reach for something to offer back. I simply listened, and he felt heard.

Eventually, slowly and not without discomfort, I began to see what I was doing. I was managing conversations, shaping them carefully, listening with one ear while another part of me prepared what to say next, something helpful or wise, just insightful enough to prove I belonged in the exchange.

I wasn't present in the moment. I was being strategic.

My mind stayed a step ahead, always composing the next empathetic reflection, rehearsing how to steer the moment toward clarity or closure. That was when the realization began to settle in. Waiting to speak is not the same as listening, and even offering loving, thoughtful advice does not mean you have truly heard someone. Understanding another person's experience, no matter how deeply, does not guarantee they have felt received.

Because real listening, the kind that allows someone to exhale, is not only about understanding but about connection, and connection does not rest on attention alone. It asks us to show up fully, open and steady, without defense.

This kind of presence cannot be performed. It is not a practiced lean-in or a well-timed nod but something quieter, willing to let go of control. It does not rescue or redirect or explain away what is unfolding. It stays.

It asks for stillness in the face of discomfort. A willingness to remain inside the uncertainty. To let the story stay unresolved, unpolished, unrescued, and to be there anyway.

Introduction

That was what I'd been missing all along.

Not because I did not care, I cared deeply, but because I was uneasy with silence, with sadness, with the raw helplessness that rises when you realize there are some things you cannot fix, that there is a kind of pain which does not need to be solved but only seen.

If I was honest, I was not trying to soothe their pain at all, I was trying to manage my own.

Once I could feel that, not only understand it but sense it in the tightness of my chest and in the way I filled space when things grew quiet, something in me began to shift. There was no fanfare, no sudden transformation, only a soft turning, like the way morning enters a room. Not all at once, and never with announcement, but simply as light arriving in degrees.

One day, almost without noticing, I looked up and realized the dark was no longer all there. At first I did not recognize it. What woke me was not something I did, but something I felt.

I would be the one speaking, letting something half-formed spill out, soft around the edges and still unsure of its own shape. Almost before the words had settled, a response would arrive in the form of advice, a suggestion, a gentle reframe, or a story about how they had handled something similar. Sometimes it came cloaked in warmth, sometimes in logic, but always too soon, before I was ready, before I had even fully arrived in what I was trying to say.

I was not asking for answers. What I needed was a place to land, a pause, a moment of being met exactly where I was.

Instead, I would leave with that familiar sense of distance, not hurt exactly, just empty, as though I had held something out and watched it get swept into someone else's meaning before it had a chance to find ground. In the quiet that followed, a question surfaced, sharp and unsettling in its clarity.

Is this what it feels like when people open up to me?

It lodged itself deep, and once it was there I could not unhear it or unsee the subtle ways I might have done the same. The recognition did not come all at once but crept in slowly, and not without discomfort.

It showed up in conversations with my partner, the kind where I believed I was being supportive, even loving, but where she felt something else entirely. I would offer a perspective, a soft reframe, something I thought might help, yet almost the moment the words left my mouth I would feel it, that subtle tightening in my chest, a quiet unease I could not quite explain.

There was no outburst and no confrontation, only a small shift in her posture, the way her shoulders turned slightly away, not in anger but in resignation, and I knew then that I had missed her again because I was not making space for her experience, I was trying to manage it.

Introduction

There was one afternoon I will not forget. I was walking past my eldest son's room. He was eleven then, in that in-between place where emotions arrive in full force but the words to carry them have not yet caught up. His door was slightly open, and I could see him sitting at the edge of his bed, hunched forward with his fists between his knees, folded in on himself as if he wanted to disappear without moving.

I paused in the doorway. "You okay, buddy?"

No response.

I stepped in a little further, softening my voice. "Hey... talk to me."

Still nothing, just a small shake of the head. After a long silence he said, "I'm fine."

But it was not the kind of *fine* that pushes people away. It was the kind that leaves the door ajar, quietly saying, *I don't know how to talk about it, please don't make me, but stay.*

Everything in me wanted to fix it, to draw him out, to say something that would make it better, yet something held me back. Whether it was grace, practice, or simply fatigue I cannot be sure, but I know I did not move toward the problem and I did not reach for an answer.

I sat down, not beside him but close enough. "Can I sit here for a bit?" I asked. He nodded.

So I did. I went quiet, not with the kind of silence that waits for an opening but with the kind that offers steady presence without asking for anything in return, the kind that says *I'm here, and you don't need to be anything but yourself.* I let my breath settle, allowed the tension to ease from my body, and let the silence stretch, not as something to be filled but as something whole. We sat like that for five minutes, maybe less, saying nothing, simply resting in the quiet hum of being near.

Then something in him softened.

His body released, his chin lifted slightly, and in a voice that barely reached me he said he did not feel sad anymore. Then he stood and went to find his brother. There was no explanation and no summary, only that quiet, unspoken return to himself, and in that moment something settled in me as well. It was not a thought but a knowing that he had not needed answers, or even words.

What he needed was space, space for his feelings to exist without being reshaped, space where he did not have to translate himself in order to be received, a moment where he could be messy, uncertain, silent, and still feel held. That stayed with me. The power wasn't in what was said but in what wasn't. In that silence he found something most of us spend a lifetime searching for, a stillness that asked nothing in return.

I see now that I had been moving through life with good intentions but bad habits. Whenever someone came to me with a problem, whether a friend, a colleague, or someone I loved, my mind would flick on, scanning the terrain. What should I say? How could I help? How could I lighten whatever felt heavy, even if only by a little? I

Introduction

thought that was empathy, but it was not. Not really. It was something else entirely, my discomfort disguised as care.

Whenever I sensed sadness I tried to lift it. If I heard confusion I reached to organize it, and when anger surfaced I moved quickly to smooth it away. I told myself this was compassion, but underneath it was resistance, resistance to what is raw, what cannot be fixed, what lingers in the long, uncertain silence that opens when you stop pretending someone's pain needs your solution, because most of the time it doesn't.

It does not need managing, it needs witnessing. And strangely, when I saw that, I did not feel ashamed, I felt curious. What would it mean to stay, not to fix or redirect, not to grasp for something meaningful to say, but simply to remain present? What would it look like to stop turning someone's ache into a puzzle I felt responsible for solving, to let silence stand without treating it as a void that demanded my voice, to stop mistaking discomfort for a call to action?

So I began to practice, not gracefully but with the awkwardness of trying something unfamiliar. It felt like moving through a darkened room, reaching out and brushing again and again against my own reflexes. My mind kept offering its usual responses, the well-worn scripts, tidy reframes, and polished reassurances that always seemed ready to be delivered. I had to learn to notice them and let them pass, to feel them rise and move through without engagement, like strangers I could acknowledge without inviting in, and in that hesitation something began to shift.

When I stopped steering conversations, they found their own current. At times they drifted, at times they stalled, yet they moved with a kind of honesty I had not known how to make room for. And when I stopped offering answers, people began to offer more of themselves, not because I pulled it from them but because I stepped out of the way.

When I stopped trying to be useful, people began to trust me, not because I had anything particularly wise to give but because they could sense I was not performing. I was no longer trying to shape their pain into something I could explain or working to contain their experience within the edges of my own understanding. I was simply there.

I began to realize that this was the work, not to fix or impress but simply to hold, and as I learned to hold others more gently, something in me softened as well. My nervous system began to settle and I no longer braced every time emotion entered the room. I stopped treating vulnerability like fire, something dangerous to be contained, and began to see it more like weather, unpredictable, transient, sometimes intense, yet not inherently threatening. I did not need to run from it. I could learn to stand inside it, not always perfectly but more often, with breath, with tenderness, with a stillness that did not need to be heroic, and over time that changed everything.

This book is the result of that shift. It does not follow a straight line or offer a perfect map. It is a trail of moments, many of them small and quiet, that only revealed their meaning once I slowed down enough to

Introduction

notice. It is not a book of advice, and you will not find five steps, communication hacks, or neatly drawn diagrams. What you will find is not a manual, but a practice.

A collection of stories, reflections, and silences, an attempt to return to something we have misplaced, or perhaps only forgotten. It is a way of being with one another without reaching for control, a way of holding space without feeling the need to fill it, and a way of listening not only with our ears but with the full weight of our attention, steady, embodied, and unhurried.

Real listening does not live in the words themselves. It lives in the spaces between them, in the breath that separates one sentence from the next, in the pause that follows "I'm fine," and in the subtle shift of someone's posture when they almost say something more. It shows up in the nervous system, in the softening of your shoulders, in the quiet steadiness of your gaze, and in the message your attention carries without a sound, the quiet assurance that says you are here, you are not leaving, even if this becomes difficult.

You do not have to become a therapist, retreat to a monastery, or master the perfect phrase. You do not need a polished response or a rehearsed technique. What matters is learning to stop reaching.

Allow the silence to breathe and let the story remain unresolved. Show the other person, not through words but through your stillness, that they are safe to be fully human in your company.

If you can do that, even for a moment, you may begin to see what I did. The most powerful conversations often do not sound like anything at all, and the deepest kind of support is quiet, even wordless. When we stop trying to be insightful or impressive or helpful, and release the need to always offer something, a different kind of presence begins to take shape in the space we have left open, something quieter, more grounded, more real.

In that space, we become the kind of person others can truly speak to, not because we always know what to say, but because we have learned how to stay with the question, with the silence, and with whatever arrives.

Part I: Noise

Chapter 1.

A call to listen

I had always wanted to learn a martial art, not for the belts or the bravado, and not because I was chasing victory, danger, or the illusion of control. Even as a child I sensed that something quieter lived inside that kind of training, something almost sacred, though I would not have named it that at the time. It felt like stillness folded inside movement, attention carried within form. Yet I never made space for it. My life was already crowded with hockey, athletics, and music practice, my body in constant motion and my calendar forever recovering.

The martial arts I saw on television were loud and performed, full of high kicks and shouting, more theatrical than real, noise dressed up as power. I did not have the words for it, but I think I was already searching for something inward, something closer to a prayer than a punch.

Years later, when I had the opportunity to move to Japan, that old longing came with me, carried not in language but in the body, folded quietly into the luggage of my life.

Shut Up — A journey into the lost art of listening

I was twenty-eight, carrying a backpack, a skateboard, and a guitar. Melbourne had begun to feel like repetition, the same streets and the same conversations, a loop that no longer opened into anything new. Something in me had stalled, and although I wasn't running, I knew I needed movement. I was restless enough to leave yet steady enough to see I could not keep living in the same way. I was not chasing martial arts but chasing aliveness.

Tokyo has its own kind of rhythm, tight, polished, and precise, everything choreographed to the minute, clean and efficient yet beautifully indifferent. It feels like breath held too long and motion without pause. I was swept up quickly in design work, music, freelance projects, and Japanese language classes, looking for a sense of belonging I did not yet feel. Each day ended with long commutes on crowded trains where we stood together in silence, perfectly contained, perfectly exhausted.

I met Junko through another Aussie expat who had offered me a job as a designer. She was quiet in a way that never asked to be noticed, not shy but carefully calibrated, and she spoke the way she chose her music, with wit, with care, and with a taste for melancholy, mostly Britpop with some Radiohead woven in. She loved cats, laughed in unexpected moments, and never explained herself, and she did not try to be anything, which more than anything else was what drew me in.

Only later did I learn that her family carried deep roots in the Japanese arts, revealed not through confession but in the way important things emerge slowly, as if waiting to see whether you are truly paying attention.

One evening she invited me to her family home outside Nagoya, where we sat at a low wooden table in *seiza*, the upright kneeling position that straightens the spine without demand. Her parents were gracious and unhurried, offering no performance of hospitality, only a quiet kind of welcome that asked nothing in return.

After dinner her father turned to me and asked if I would like to see their dojo. I bowed slightly and answered, "*Hai*, yes."

We drove a short distance through quiet streets that seemed to soften under the evening light. The building we stopped at looked unremarkable, its weathered metal siding and flickering fluorescent bulb framed by a rusted sign that hinted it had once been a mechanic's shop. A narrow staircase was tucked behind the structure, the metal railing cool and slightly rough beneath my hand as we climbed. At the top waited a plain wooden door, its edges worn smooth, and he opened it without a word.

Inside there was stillness, not the kind that demands silence but the kind that is silence itself.

Tatami mats stretched across the floor in gentle symmetry, their weave softened by decades of quiet footsteps. Along one wall stood a row of wooden weapons in perfect alignment, each one placed with intention, waiting. Above them hung calligraphy scrolls that carried not decoration but quiet declarations of lineage and devotion. The room did not feel empty, it felt held in suspension, as if a breath had been drawn in and never quite released.

Her father walked to the center of the room and lifted a naginata, the traditional pole weapon once used by samurai, its long wooden shaft ending in a gently curved blade. He stood for a moment, not poised for action but settled into something quieter, as if he were listening, or remembering, or simply arriving. Then he began to move.

What unfolded did not feel like performance but ritual, each arc of the blade tracing something precise yet unseen, each step landing with the weight of punctuation. His body moved like calligraphy, fluid, deliberate, and entirely unforced. Then, without warning, he turned toward me, stepping forward fast and silent, the blade sweeping through the air until it stopped just inches from my face. He held it there, unwavering, his eyes fixed on mine, carrying no aggression and no challenge, only a presence that was full and unmistakable.

A moment later he lowered the blade and bowed, and I bowed back. Nothing was spoken, yet something unmistakable had been communicated, complete and wordless. Perhaps part of it was a warning not to mess with his daughter, but what passed between us went deeper than that.

It was my first real lesson in martial arts, and it had nothing to do with fighting. It was about quiet authority, the kind that does not announce itself or rely on noise or force to be felt, the kind that changes the shape of a room simply by entering it.

A call to listen

I did not begin training right away. Life was still noisy, and I remained distracted, carried by the inertia of work, commutes, and obligations. Yet something in me had shifted. It was not dramatic or easily defined, but it was unmistakable, like a current beneath the surface quietly beginning to change direction. And as with most things worth following, it did not arrive with certainty. There was no grand insight or clear decision, only a feeling that was subtle, persistent, and unshakable, a quiet knowing that settled in and refused to leave.

It would take time before I understood what had started that night, but the truth of it had already begun to take root, in my body, in the silence, in the space he carved with that blade and with that stillness. It was the beginning of something, a way of listening I had not known I was missing.

The noise we swim in

I stayed in Japan for almost six years. When Junko and I returned to Australia, I expected to feel grounded again, as if crossing that threshold back into familiar air, familiar streets, and familiar voices would finally let me exhale. For a while I did, finding comfort in the known and a quiet relief in moving through social rhythms without effort. Yet beneath that familiarity something had shifted, and I realized it was not the country that had changed, it was me.

Everything moved faster than I remembered. Conversations were plentiful and often warm, yet many seemed to skim the surface, animated but scattered. People spoke quickly and often, but their attention felt fractured, divided by something I could not quite name.

By 2010 the shift had a name, the attention economy. The iPhone was no longer a novelty, Facebook had gone global, and tweets were everywhere. Social media was no longer something you visited, it had become something you lived inside, a constant current carried in your pocket.

At first it felt expansive, full of possibility, a permanent open door to everyone and everything. But gradually, almost without notice, it began to feel like noise.

I remember sitting in a café one morning, watching the room around me. Every table was filled with friends, couples, and coworkers, yet hardly anyone was speaking. Heads were bowed not in reverence but in habit, thumbs moving rhythmically across screens, eyes glazed and unfocused. People were together, but not truly with each other.

I could feel it taking hold in me as well.

At home I often caught myself mid-scroll, drawn into threads where strangers argued over politics, parenting, and spirituality, topics none of us were truly equipped to resolve. Each post felt like a performance, every reply carrying the weight of quiet defense. It was all signal without anchor, a chorus of voices speaking at once, yet no one was really listening.

The more I participated, the more fragmented I became, and gradually it began to bleed into real conversations. I noticed myself interrupting more, not out of impatience but anticipation, jumping in halfway through someone's sentence, eager to contribute, to steer the moment before it slipped away. I no longer let people finish or allowed silences to unfold. Without realizing it, I had started to treat dialogue like a digital thread, something to manage and optimize, as if I were moderating a comment section rather than sitting across from someone I loved.

It was subtle, but my body knew. My nervous system leaned forward, always a few beats ahead, composing replies, framing impressions, managing my attention rather than inhabiting it. I was present, but not fully, caught in a web of alerts, opinions, and expectations. The most dangerous part was that I did not notice it happening.

That is the thing about erosion, it does not arrive with fanfare. It moves slowly and quietly, wearing down the edges until, one day, you realize that something you believed was whole has already been hollowed out.

By 2014 I reached a quiet threshold. There was no grand decision, no moment of announcing to the world that I was stepping away from social media, no declaration at all. I was simply tired of it.

So I let it go.

I closed my accounts and turned off notifications, letting the noise fall silent, not as a gesture or to prove anything, but because I felt as if I were drowning in something I could not name. What I needed was space, and what I craved was air, and in that quiet something returned. It came without drama or speed, only gently, a flicker of what I had not realized was missing, my attention. And with it came my capacity to listen, not only to words but to tone, to breath, to the pauses that carry meaning between sentences, to the presence of the person in front of me.

There is research to support this. Studies confirm what many of us feel but struggle to name, that constant digital engagement reduces empathy. Even the silent presence of a phone on the table can lower the quality of connection, and "phubbing," the act of checking a phone mid-conversation, does more than break attention, it breaks trust.

You do not need studies to know this, because you have felt it. That moment of disconnection when someone drops their gaze while you are talking. They may say they are listening, perhaps even believe they are, but something shifts. It is small yet significant, and something breaks.

Once, just to test it, I changed the subject mid-sentence when someone glanced at their phone in response to that all-too-familiar notification ping. When they looked back up they smiled and nodded, pretending they had been listening the whole time, unaware the topic had shifted. In those few seconds they had not only missed a few words, they might as well have left the room.

That was when it truly landed for me, that real listening does not survive in distraction. It is not only about hearing, it is about staying, and in a world built to fracture our focus, staying is no longer instinctive. It has become a choice, a skill, and at times even a quiet rebellion.

It started with a mop

I still remember the day I met Sensei.

It was the year we had just returned from Japan and life was beginning to settle, or at least giving the appearance of it. Our first child was on the way, and something inside me began to stir. It was not panic or fear but something quieter, a subtle tug beneath the surface, a sense that before stepping into this new chapter I needed to root myself, not simply prepare or plan but anchor.

For reasons I could not fully explain, I knew that anchor needed to include something Japanese, not for nostalgia or aesthetics but as a thread, a way to stay tethered to the part of myself I did not want to lose in the transition to fatherhood. It was the part that had changed in Japan, the part that had seen stillness up close and been marked by it. So I began looking for a dojo.

There were a few nearby, but one name stood out to me, World Aikido Yoga. The combination gave me pause. Aikido I understood, but yoga brought to mind incense, whale sounds, and stretchy pants, not exactly the peaceful warrior path I had imagined. Still, something nudged me forward, and I went.

I arrived early, far too early, a habit I had not yet grown out of. The street was quiet and the door still locked, so I stood outside, rehearsing what I might say, unsure of what I was stepping into. Then a man approached, compact and steady, moving without hurry. He did not smile, only looked at me, not with suspicion but with attention, the kind of look you give the sky when you are trying to read the weather.

"You must be the new guy," he said as he unlocked the door. Without breaking stride he added, "There's the floor mop. Start cleaning the floor."

That was it. No handshake, no tour, no introduction to what Aikido was or why I might want to train. Just a tool and a task.

Leaning against the wall was a long-handled dust mop, the kind used for sweeping broad wooden floorboards, wide enough to cover five at a time. The wooden staff was darkened at the grip from years of hands doing exactly what I was now being asked to do. So I mopped.

A call to listen

There were no instructions and no supervision, only me and the empty room. I moved slowly across the floorboards, the mop gliding ahead of me in long, deliberate strokes. Up and back, clearing the space before the mats could be laid down. I did not know where to begin or when I would be finished, only that the motion made sense, and somewhere in its rhythm something in me began to settle, a quiet kind of centering.

I did not know it at the time, but that was the first lesson.

There is something quietly radical about being asked to clean a space before you are invited into it. It humbles you, recalibrates the nervous system, and sends a message without a word that this is not a place to take from but a place to tend. And that matters, because if you are not willing to care for the ground, you are not ready to stand on it.

At the time I did not have those words. I was simply trying not to look lost. Yet as I cleaned the floor, a thought passed through me, fleeting but insistent. Maybe this is what fatherhood is.

Not the big speeches or the carefully prepared wisdom, but the quiet, unglamorous work of preparation that begins long before anyone else arrives. The noticing of what no one else sees, the clearing of space before the room is filled, and the steady act of holding the ground, not for control or recognition but simply because it matters.

Cleaning that floor taught me more than I expected. It showed me that listening does not begin with the ears but with humility, attention, and the willingness to tend to the spaces that hold the weight of others, often long before they ever speak. Sometimes the most sacred things begin with nothing more than mopping the floor.

The sound before the listening

Looking back now, I can see how the threads began to weave, the mopping, the silence, the stepping away. At the time they felt like separate moments, small and almost forgettable. But change does not always announce itself. Sometimes it begins as a quiet ache, a subtle tightening you cannot name, a shift in gravity, or the sense that something no longer fits the way it once did.

What I felt was not exhaustion in the usual sense. It was quieter, more insidious, as if the air around me had thickened, as if presence had become something I had to push through rather than a place I could rest, not only physically but existentially.

I began to feel it in places that once felt like home, in conversations, in projects, in familiar rooms. I was still showing up and saying the right things, but something essential was not arriving with me. I was there, but not fully, as if I had begun performing myself.

A call to listen

In conversation I caught myself offering advice no one had asked for. In meetings I filled silences too quickly, afraid they might be mistaken for uncertainty. In friendships I confused talking with intimacy and certainty with care.

Online the noise only intensified. Every news article and every comment I read felt like part of an endless performance, not only of opinion but of identity, each person curating a take, broadcasting belief, presenting a polished self. The volume kept rising, yet the listening had disappeared.

I began to feel thin, not metaphorically and not in any luminous or translucent way, but worn. Frayed at the edges, as if my nervous system had been pulled in too many directions for too long and the strands were beginning to give.

So I stepped back, not dramatically, but quietly. I walked a little more, spent less time reading the news, and allowed more silence. I had no plan and was not seeking transformation, I simply needed to breathe again. And in that space something unexpected surfaced, not insight or clarity but stillness.

At first it was barely perceptible, a jaw unclenching, a breath I had not realized I was holding, or a thought left unfinished because it no longer needed to be tied up. I could hear myself again, not clearly but in fragments, and that was enough.

Slowly a new question began to form. What if listening was not something I needed to do, but something I needed to become? Not a technique to master but a posture to inhabit, not a skillset but a way of moving through the world.

That understanding did not arrive all at once. It came in flickers, in the quiet that followed a real question, in the softening of my son's shoulders when I stayed close without trying to fix, in the rhythm of cleaning a floor, in the restraint of holding back one more clever insight and letting the moment breathe.

There is a sound that comes before listening. You cannot name it exactly. It is not quite a sound but a shift, something in the pressure of the room, a loosening in the body, a small interior door swinging quietly open. It arrives when you stop tracking, stop composing, stop shaping what comes next, when you let go of where it is going and allow yourself to be fully here without condition. That is how it began for me, not with mastery or understanding but with something quieter, with surrender.

Chapter 2.
Why people don't need your opinion

When was the last time someone gave you advice you did not ask for? Not because you were lost or looking for help, but because you were speaking out loud, trying to make sense of something as you went. Maybe it happened after a hard day, when your child said something that left you hollow, or your boss blindsided you in a meeting, or you just felt off in a way you could not explain. So you told someone. A friend, a partner, a colleague. They meant well, truly, as they leaned in and said, "You know what you should do?"

Maybe what they offered was sound or wise, something practical or kind. Yet something in you pulled back, not with offense or drama, but with a quiet withdrawal so subtle it might have gone unnoticed, even by you. The problem was not the advice itself but the moment it arrived, too early, before you were ready, before the ache had formed enough shape to be named. It missed something essential, not only the context, but the deeper part of you that needed to be heard first.

I have been on both sides of that moment. I have offered opinions, believing I was being helpful or generous, and I have also been on the receiving end, when what I truly needed was something much quieter. Not advice, not solutions, just company. A stillness beside me. The kind of attention that does not rush to reshape what I have not yet finished saying, and the truth is, neither side feels good.

There was a time, several years after I had sold my business, when my partner was in the early stages of building one of her own. She would talk through the inevitable challenges, whether it was a difficult client, a dip in cash flow, or a campaign that didn't land the way she had hoped. I tried to listen, I truly did, but somewhere in the middle of her speaking, I would feel it rising, a slow nudge in the chest, the tightening just behind the eyes.

I recognized the terrain and thought, I can help. So I began, gently and thoughtfully, with love. I offered ideas, reframed the problem, suggested next steps. Not because I didn't care, but because I did. She never argued or snapped back, but eventually the look would come. Quiet. Steady. Unmistakable. A gaze that stopped me mid-sentence and said everything without needing to speak. *I don't need your opinion right now. I need you to hold the space.*

In that moment, I saw it. I saw myself from the outside, standing there with all my careful advice, all my good intentions, all my experience laid bare. None of it unkind. None of it exactly wrong. Just slightly off. Out of tune with what was truly needed.

Why people don't need your opinion

It is hard not to give your opinion, especially when it feels like an offering, especially when it comes from love. But what is harder, quieter, and more difficult to name is sitting across from someone who is not really listening. When someone listens only to respond, their attention begins to narrow, and their presence starts to fracture. You can feel it. That subtle shift from being with you to trying to fix you.

Often, the most generous thing we can offer is not our wisdom or even our opinion, but our willingness to stay. To remain present without needing to shape, to solve, or to step in front of what is still unfolding. It means letting someone be exactly where they are, without hurrying them toward where we believe they should be.

We live in a culture that is addicted to being right, where opinions are no longer just ideas but have become identities. We defend them like territory and broadcast them like brands. We expect others not only to listen, but to agree or accept correction.

Social media did not create this impulse, but it amplified it. It taught us to respond instantly, speak loudly, and stay visible. Every hashtag, every post, every hot take became a kind of performance, carefully curated to be liked, shared, and followed. We learned how to broadcast our beliefs, but very few of us learned how to listen, especially when we do not agree, when we do not understand, or when someone is in pain and we have no idea what to say.

That was when I began to notice it in myself. The reflex to fill silence with something useful, anything at all. An opinion, a suggestion, a personal story. Not because I didn't care, but because I did. I wanted to ease their discomfort, or maybe just my own.

I meant well, as most of us do, but good intentions are not the same as good impact. When someone is hurting, what they often need is not insight but undivided attention. They want to feel heard before they are advised, understood before they are fixed, and respected before they are reshaped.

What makes this difficult is how quietly it happens. We believe we are connecting, helping, sharing, and in some ways we are, but only in part. Real connection does not depend on agreement. It depends on being seen, and to truly see someone, especially when their experience is different from our own, requires a slower, more spacious kind of listening. Not the kind that waits politely for its turn to speak, but the kind that holds still and makes room. The kind that says, without rushing to respond, I am here, and I do not need to change you.

Once I began to notice this, I could not unsee it. That kind of listening had become rare, in homes, in relationships, in workplaces. It felt especially absent online, where silence is often mistaken for weakness and anonymity invites judgment. We have stopped asking questions and instead rush to correct, to assume, to declare. And in doing so, we lose something deeply human.

A few years ago, I made a promise to myself not to offer my opinion unless someone asked for it. At first, it felt unnatural, almost like withholding, as if staying silent meant abandoning the people I cared about. But over time, something shifted. People began to open up more. They lingered in conversation and told the truth more freely, not because I had the right answers, but because I stopped trying to give any.

Instead of offering advice, I began to ask questions. Sincere ones.

How do you think you'll handle it? What's the toughest part right now? How are you feeling about it?

And gradually, something softened. People no longer felt managed or assessed, and they did not feel interrupted or steered toward a solution. They felt met in their experience, not fixed or redirected, but simply accompanied.

Isn't that what most of us are really looking for? Not to be corrected, but to be held in our complexity, just as we are, without being edited.

This is not about silencing yourself, and it is not about holding back your truth. It is about restraint, the kind that comes from humility, from curiosity, from the quiet understanding that presence often matters more than perspective. Most people do not need your opinion as much as they need space. Space to hear themselves.

Space to feel without explanation. Space to trust their own voice, simply because yours had the grace to wait.

Drowning in opinions

In today's hyper-connected world, unsolicited opinions have become part of the background noise of daily life. They are not limited to social media. They show up at dinner tables, in meeting rooms, on sidewalks. A steady current of commentary runs beneath it all, creating a quiet but persistent pressure to respond, to take a stance, to offer a take and be ready to defend it.

But this is not just a cultural annoyance, it has real consequences. The more saturated we become with noise, the harder it becomes to hear anything meaningful. Not just each other, but even ourselves.

During Melbourne's long and surreal COVID-19 lockdowns, the city settled into an eerie stillness. Streets emptied, playgrounds grew quiet, and faces disappeared behind masks. But the stillness was not peaceful. It carried a weight. Beneath it was grief, and fear, and a deep fatigue. A kind of collective fraying that could be felt but not easily named.

Why people don't need your opinion

When that pressure finally broke, it did not release through dialogue. It broke open through division. Suddenly, everyone had an opinion, and most of them were loud.

Online, it was constant. Article after article, thread after thread, each one filled with comments that were not just full of disagreement, but saturated with certainty. Identity was being performed through positions, and outrage had begun to feel like a form of belonging. What had once been a space for connection now felt more like an arena, where the goal was no longer understanding but dominance. Sides were not just taken. They were drawn as if preparing for battle.

What struck me most was not the rage online, but the silence offline. Or more precisely, the absence of curiosity.

I remember watching a downtown protest. On one side of the street, people rallied against lockdowns and vaccine mandates, while on the other, a counter-protest had formed. The air was thick with signs, shouting, and police barriers. Then, from one side, a chant began to rise.

"If you don't want the vax, you can go and get f#@ked!"

It was not just the language that landed with force. It was the flatness of it, the complete collapse of wonder. No one was listening. No one was even trying to understand. That was when it hit me with its full weight. We had begun to treat real life the way we treat comment sections, not just divided, but dehumanized. Everything had become tribal, reactive, and armored.

This was no longer just a public health emergency. It had become a crisis in how we relate to one another. The digital world had trained us to equate disagreement with threat, to compress complexity into slogans, and to replace conversation with spectacle. The cost of this shift was high. Communities fractured, relationships frayed, and even the simple act of being in a real conversation began to feel rare. We were no longer showing up as people but as positions.

Families stopped speaking, workplaces grew tense and fragile, and friends drifted into silence. Not because they stopped caring, but because they were afraid. They were afraid of being wrong, of being misunderstood, or of being dismissed. That sense of dismissal became the water we swam in, embedded in headlines, threaded through sarcasm, and echoed in every performative post insisting, let me tell you why you are wrong.

Something essential eroded during those years, and it was not only trust in the systems around us. It was trust in each other. I still wonder how different things could have been. Maybe not entirely changed, but softened, if more people had simply paused before reacting. Paused before hitting send, before crossing their arms, before picking a side. If even one person had stepped off the curb, crossed the street, and asked with real sincerity: *Can you tell me why this matters so much to you?*

Not to debate. Not to win. Not to correct. Just to listen.

Opinions are loud, but they are rarely truly heard. Beneath even the most forcefully delivered words, there is often something much quieter. A core of fear, grief, confusion, or longing that remains unseen. None of it can surface if we are only preparing our rebuttal. In the end, we were not drowning under the weight of too many opinions, but because no one was listening.

The psychological impact of unsolicited advice

Unsolicited advice, the kind we offer without being asked, often comes from a good place. We see someone struggling, and something in us stirs. We want to help, to ease their pain, to share what worked for us, to offer something that might lighten the weight they are carrying. But research shows that this impulse, even when rooted in care, often does more harm than good. Not only to the person receiving the advice, but to the relationship itself.

Psychologists Eran Magen and Bo Feng have studied this dynamic closely and found that unsolicited advice most often arises in close relationships, between friends, partners, parents, and children.[2] We offer it because we care, but the very closeness that moves us to speak can also make the advice feel intrusive. What was meant as comfort can lead to defensiveness, and what was meant as reassurance can create distance.

When someone is vulnerable, naming grief, fear, or frustration, and the first response they hear is "You should..." or "Have you tried...?", it rarely feels like support. No matter how well-intentioned, it often lands as something else entirely. Something that feels more like quiet management, a soft judgment, or a gentle dismissal of what is still raw.

Sarah, a young mother from Melbourne, described this exact experience on a blog. She had finally allowed herself to open up during a conversation with a friend, sharing the quiet pressure that had been building, the tug-of-war between career and motherhood, and the relentless sense of falling short in both. She wasn't asking for advice, only for a place to set down her exhaustion without needing to explain it. But her friend, eager to help, responded with a stream of solutions including time-blocking strategies, meal prep ideas, and a list of meditation apps.

"You just need to be more organized," she said, with a smile.

Sarah smiled too, but inside, something went quiet. It was not a feeling of support, but of being reduced, as if her struggle had been shrunk into a scheduling issue and she herself had become a problem to solve.

Why people don't need your opinion

Advice, even when it is good, can feel like criticism when it arrives uninvited. The brain, wired for both autonomy and safety, often hears it as a subtle threat. A quiet message beneath the surface that says, you can't handle this, or let me take over.

Psychologists call this reactance, a motivational state that arises when we feel our freedom is being limited or questioned. It helps explain why people sometimes resist the very thing that might help them. Not because the advice is wrong, but because it was not earned. It was imposed.

The real issue is not advice itself, but the timing, the trust, and the delicate dynamics of control that surface when we try to help too soon. Often, our urge to advise is not only about easing another person's pain. It is also about soothing our own discomfort with what we cannot fix. So we rush to speak, to offer, to organize, and in doing so, we overlook the deeper need to be seen before being guided, and to be met before being managed.

What fosters connection, what allows people to soften and open, is not answers but undivided attention. The kind of quiet focus that does not steer or interrupt. The kind that listens not to respond but to witness, and that says, without agenda or urgency, I'm not here to fix you. I'm here with you.

Over time, unsolicited advice teaches people to hold back. They begin to shrink the parts of themselves that do not fit neatly into a solution. They stop reaching out, because what is raw keeps getting reshaped into something more palatable for someone else. Slowly, they learn to stay silent, not out of strength, but out of self-protection.

The hard truth is that uninvited advice often serves the giver more than the receiver. It offers us something to do, a role to step into, and a sense of control that helps us feel useful, capable, and needed. While all of that is deeply human, it is not the same as love. Love asks for something more difficult. It asks us to stay close without taking over, to hold steady even when silence stretches, to witness what is unresolved without rushing to fix it, and to offer presence instead of strategy.

The role of social media in amplifying opinions

If unsolicited advice has always been part of human nature, social media has turned it into an epidemic. Not so long ago, having an opinion meant sharing it in conversation, around a dinner table, at the pub, in the kitchen after a long day. An opinion had a face, a tone, a rhythm shaped by breath and pause, and the unspoken energy of being in the same room. Now we are expected to have an opinion about everything, instantly, publicly, and decisively.

Why people don't need your opinion

Platforms like YouTube, Facebook, Instagram, Reddit, and X did not invent the human need to be seen and heard, but they scaled it, industrialized it, and turned it into a system of validation. A kind of scoreboard for identity that rewards not reflection but immediacy, not nuance but certainty, not listening but performance.

You do not need to be informed, only emphatic. You do not need to stay curious, only loud. And if your outrage is sharp enough, the algorithm will amplify it. That constant invitation to broadcast has reshaped how we show up in the world. We now share not only more, but faster and louder, with less context, less care, and more urgency to prove we are paying attention.

The result is not clarity but static. A low-grade emotional hum that drowns out depth. A kind of noise so thick that the quieter truths, the ones that require breath and pause and presence, can barely make it through.

Psychologists have begun studying this with increasing urgency. A 2024 study in *Frontiers in Psychology* found that compulsive social media use and information overload are strong predictors of what they call social media fatigue. This is a psychological state marked not only by distraction but also by anxiety, guilt, and emotional withdrawal. Participants did not simply feel overwhelmed by content, they felt crushed by the expectation to respond, to comment, to react, to stay visible. And when they did not, the absence of activity brought not relief but a creeping sense of irrelevance.[3]

Another influential study, published in *Public Opinion Quarterly*, examined how online exposure to polarizing commentary shapes outlook. The findings were revealing. Participants who read identical articles alongside comment threads expressed more extreme views than those who saw the same content without comments. As perspectives hardened, empathy diminished and curiosity began to fade. People shifted from arriving open-minded to arriving emotionally armored. Because when everyone is speaking and no one is listening, it no longer feels safe to be unsure, to pause, or to say, "I don't know."[4]

You have probably seen this, even today, in that moment during a conversation when someone reaches for their phone. They may not mean anything by it, yet it still says something. Something small but cumulative. It says, this moment we are in can wait.

We have normalized it. The glance away, the distracted nod, the scrolling during silence. Yet research is clear that even these subtle acts of divided attention erode connection, not because they are aggressive, but because they are ambient, a thousand quiet signals saying, I'm not fully here. Over time, those signals do more than hurt, they begin to rewire us.

Social media has given us more ways to speak and more channels to reach across, but it has not taught us how to listen. If anything, it has made listening harder. We have been trained to react before we reflect, to perform rather than pause, to speak loudly, publicly, and relentlessly before we have even asked what truly wants to be said.

That training does not stay online. It walks into our kitchens, our meetings, and the spaces that once held breath and room for change. Connection does not begin with declaration but with attention, the kind that listens without rushing, that notices what is left unsaid, that waits long enough to sense what lives beneath the words. Beneath all the hot takes and unsolicited opinions, under the cleverness and the noise, there is a quieter longing that remains. The desire to be heard before we are corrected. To be understood before we are improved. And right now, for many of us, that need is going unmet.

Active, reflective and empathetic listening

If speaking has become our default, then listening has quietly become an endangered skill. It is strange when you think about it, because listening should be simple. It does not require credentials or charisma, and you do not need to be persuasive, articulate, or clever. You do not even need to agree. Yet the kind of listening that makes someone feel safe, truly seen and held in their humanness, has grown rare. It is so rare that when we encounter it, we remember it for years, because it feels so different from what we usually receive.

Most of the time, what passes for listening is little more than waiting for our turn to speak. We nod politely while composing our next sentence, scanning for the moment we can jump in. We say, "I know exactly how you feel," and then shift to our own story, our pain, our punchline. And while we mean well, it is not malice that drives us. It is training. We have been taught, in quiet and persistent ways, that value lies in what we say, how quickly we can solve, how confidently we can respond, and how much we contribute to the moment. Within that framework, silence begins to feel like failure, restraint like weakness, and stillness like not enough.

Real listening is not passive, and it is not something we fall into simply because we do not know what else to do. It is active, intentional, and quietly strong, often requiring more effort than we realize. In therapeutic circles, it is often referred to as active listening, but real listening reaches beyond any single technique. It is a posture, a way of being that honors someone's inner world without inserting ourselves into it.

At its heart are three interconnected capacities: the presence of active listening, the attunement of reflective listening, and the compassion of empathic listening. Active listening draws our full attention to the speaker. Reflective listening mirrors back what we hear, not just in words but in emotional tone. Empathic listening combines these qualities to help us feel what they feel and begin to see the world through their eyes.

These practices ask us to be fully present, not just with our ears, but with our breath, our body, and our attention. They ask us to set aside the impulse to judge or fix, and instead offer stillness so the other can unfold.

Why people don't need your opinion

It means letting the other person lead the conversation, trusting that if they need our insight, they will ask for it. And if they do not, that is not a rejection, but an invitation to simply stay. More often than not, what people need is not our advice but our undivided attention.

Carl Rogers, the pioneering humanistic psychologist, called this unconditional positive regard. The experience of being deeply heard and accepted without any pressure to change. He believed this kind of listening could be transformational, not because it handed people solutions, but because it created the safety in which people could uncover their own.

Modern research supports this. In controlled studies of everyday conversations, people who received this kind of listening reported feeling more understood than those who were given advice or brief acknowledgments. That experience of being understood is what strengthens connection, deepens empathy, and builds trust. Even in brief encounters with a stranger, a colleague, or a child, the simple act of listening with presence can leave someone feeling calmer, seen, and supported.[5]

The hard part is that it takes discipline. It requires us to resist the urge to perform, to pause our instinct to manage the moment, and instead to attend to it. Real listening is not only about what we choose not to say. It is also about the texture of our silence, the steadiness of our presence, and the way we hold someone's uncertainty without flinching or rushing to smooth it over.

It shows up in quiet moments, when someone stumbles or doubts, when they almost say the thing that matters most, and we do not interrupt or redirect. We wait, and sometimes that waiting is everything. Maybe we say, "Tell me more," or simply, "That sounds hard." Or maybe we say nothing at all, offering instead a still, anchoring attention that does not need to be explained.

In a world that moves too fast, where noise is mistaken for insight and visibility for value, listening becomes a radical act. It is not passive, but deeply powerful. When we really listen, something shifts, not just in the other person, but in us. We begin to slow down, to soften, and suddenly there is more room in the conversation than we expected. More room in ourselves, and it is in that space that healing begins.

Chapter 3.

What gets in the way

In those early Aikido years, I trained obsessively. Every class I could make, I was there, and on the nights when the dojo was closed, I trained alone, chasing a feeling I did not yet have language for. When space was not available, I dragged a mattress into the garage and hung a rope from the rafters to practice high falls. I tied the jo to the ceiling and drilled parries in the half-light, sweat pooling at my feet in a kind of quiet devotion. I filled notebooks, sketched diagrams late into the night, and scribbled insights as if they were spells I had not yet learned to cast. I wanted to know everything, master it all, get it right.

But something kept jamming the signal and it wasn't my body or my schedule. It was subtler than that, something slippery and internal. A pressure in the mind, the need to be good, to prove something. Maybe to Sensei, maybe to the other students, or maybe just to the part of me that still believed worth was earned through usefulness and skill.

I remember one night when we were drilling *irimi nage*, a classic entering throw, and nothing was landing. My body was tight, my timing was off. I was rushing, thinking too far ahead, trying to execute the technique instead of feeling it.

Sensei came over, calm and patient and said, "Stop trying so hard. Let the uke teach you." Then he walked away. I didn't understand. I remember thinking, *But I'm here to learn from you.*

It took months, maybe years, for that to land. In Aikido, the uke is the one who attacks, the one who receives your technique. Let the uke teach you means letting the encounter itself become the teacher. Do not force the technique or try to lead the moment. Receive it.

That is not just Aikido. That is listening.

The biggest obstacle to real listening is not noise, or time, or even technology. It is ego, the part of us that quietly hungers to be seen as competent, wise, and valuable. It is the fear that if we do not offer something insightful, we will fade into the background. It is the discomfort that silence brings, the pressure to perform, the anxiety of not knowing what to say and being exposed in that uncertainty.

These are the real interferences, not only on the mat but in every meaningful exchange.

In the dojo, I felt it every time I tried to do the technique instead of moving with my partner. Every time I anticipated rather than received. Every time I turned the practice into a demonstration of ability instead of a meeting with the moment.

The same thing appears in conversation. We interrupt not because we are careless, but because we are afraid the moment will pass us by. We offer advice not to take control, but because we want to help, or to be seen as helpful, or simply to affirm that we still matter. We rush to fill silence not because it is empty, but because it stirs something in us we are not always ready to feel.

Silence is not a failure, and it is not the absence of meaning. It is the space where meaning begins to unfold, the uncluttered openness that allows something real to enter, whether in conversation, in conflict, or in the moment of a throw.

I did not learn this in a lecture. I learned it by getting it wrong, by noticing when I was gripping too tightly, moving too quickly, or overthinking instead of feeling. And over time, through practice and attention, I began to understand what it meant to release. To loosen my hold on needing to know, needing to teach, needing to be anything other than fully here.

What gets in the way of listening is rarely ignorance or indifference. More often, it is the quiet ache to prove that we matter. And the more we try to assert our value, the more difficult it becomes for others to feel their own.

Holding without fixing

When my second son was born, just two and a half years after my first, I thought I was ready. Not like the first time, when I paced the house with clenched hands and a racing heart, checking the hospital bag for the fifth time and wondering if I was about to become someone else. That kind of readiness had been all adrenaline and fear.

The second time was quieter, more familiar. I knew how to cradle a newborn, how to support that floppy neck with one hand while doing everything else with the other. I knew which diapers would not leak, how to tuck a blanket around him so he stayed warm but not too warm, and how to sway until he melted into that boneless sleep only babies seem to know.

I was not panicked, but I was not prepared either. At least not in the way that truly mattered. What I had not yet learned was that being prepared is not the same as being present. And presence, the real kind, does not always become easier with practice. In some ways, it becomes harder, especially when life is already full.

My partner and I passed shifts like exhausted co-pilots, juggling meals, nap schedules, and all the invisible negotiations parents come to know by necessity. Who was more tired, who had done more night feeds, who might get to rest a bit that day, and through it all, life

What gets in the way

kept moving. Work pulled at me, bills arrived without pause, and the world carried on.

Somewhere in that constant swirl, I began to drift. Not from love or responsibility, but from the weight of it all. The mental load of keeping everything spinning had begun to wear through me. I would walk into the room and see my newborn son curled on the playmat or resting in his mother's arms, and my heart would swell with love, with awe, and sometimes with guilt. Then the phone would buzz with a message from my business partner or a client needing something. The dishes would glare. Some half-formed task would surface in my mind like a missed heartbeat, and just like that, I would be gone again. Present in body, but not in spirit. Holding, but not held and he could feel it.

Babies do not need language to know when you have left. They look at you without agenda or performance, simply being, soft, wide open, entirely here. When my youngest looked at me, he was not asking for anything complicated. He just wanted me to arrive, not with solutions, not with noise, just with me.

One night I will not forget, he was crying. Not the hungry cry, not the sharp change-me cry, but that restless, unsettled kind that says, *I do not know what I need. Just stay.* I picked him up and bounced gently on the yoga ball, swaying as I had done many times before, making those soft, rhythmic sounds parents fall into like mantras. But I was not really there. My hands were on him, steady and familiar, but my mind was a storm of work, money, unfinished deadlines, the unresolved fight still echoing in the background, how much I missed sleep, and the quiet fear that I might be failing at everything all at once.

And then he stopped. Not because I found the perfect rhythm, and not because I did anything particularly right. He stopped because I did. Something in me let go, as if an invisible thread had finally released. I sat down and pulled him close, holding him against my chest, his head tucked just under my chin. His breath, fast at first, shallow and searching, began to slow, and mine did too.

In that stillness, I arrived. Not with a fix, not with a plan, but with presence. Quiet, anchoring, and unmistakably real. That moment stayed with me not because it was dramatic, but because it was everything. He felt me. I felt him. And for a brief stretch of time, the world went quiet.

What I learned that night was not something a book could have taught. No class, no clever quote could have given it shape. Being fully with someone is not what happens once the work is done. It is what makes the work matter. It is the thread that weaves everything else together, the quiet gravity at the center of connection. It is how we say, without needing a single word, I am here. I see you. You matter.

Real listening begins there. Not with ears or polished responses, but with the deep, undeniable human longing we carry from the moment we are born. The need to be received.

What gets in the way

The space between

If there is one thing I have come to understand through all the hours spent on the mat, the quiet evenings beside my sons' beds, and the awkward apologies after missing the mark in relationships, it is this.

Listening is not hard because it is complicated. It is hard because it asks us to drop everything that protects us. The very traits that help us function in the world, such as competence, speed, certainty, and even kindness, are often the same ones that quietly interfere. We want to be useful. We want to offer something of value. We want to show up well. Yet in our effort to help, we often miss what matters most, which is the simple, sacred experience of being received.

I have lost count of how many times I have interrupted someone, not out of rudeness but out of reflex. How many times I have reached for a solution when all they needed was space. How often I have nodded along, already scripting my next sentence, only to watch something fragile slip away. A blink, a breath, a half-formed truth that needed just a little more room to land.

It is not just me, it is all of us. What gets in the way of listening is rarely a lack of care. More often, it is the emotional static we carry, including the need to be right, the discomfort with silence, and the deep, often unconscious longing to feel helpful, insightful, or relevant. Our attention is under constant siege from notifications, deadlines, and the quiet weight of things left undone. We live in a world that prizes speed over depth and certainty over curiosity, and that orientation inevitably shapes how we listen. We begin to anticipate rather than receive, to assume rather than inquire. We finish each other's sentences not out of intimacy, but out of impatience.

Carl Rogers wrote that one of the most healing gifts we can offer is a presence that is accepting, nonjudgmental, and deeply understanding. Not advice. Not interpretation. Just a steady and unhurried kind of care.

Neuroscience echoes this. In studies of caregiver-child interaction, researchers have found that the calm presence of an attuned adult lowers cortisol levels, the body's primary stress hormone, and activates neural pathways associated with trust. What makes the difference is not what the caregiver says, but how they are there.

One study observed a child under stress. When a supportive adult stayed close, the child's breathing slowed, their shoulders relaxed, and their brain stopped bracing for impact. Although the research focused on developmental science, the physiological dynamics point to something more universal. Proximity and attuned presence have the power to quiet the brain's alarm system in all of us.[6]

We are each moving through the world with nervous systems quietly scanning for safety, for resonance, for someone who stays. When someone truly listens, not to

What gets in the way

evaluate or impress, but simply to be with us, something in us exhales and begins to soften. We arrive more fully. This is the quiet power of staying with another person. Not to change the moment, but to hold it gently, without pulling it out of shape.

Still, it is not easy. Not because we are incapable, but because true attentiveness requires a kind of inner spaciousness that many of us have forgotten how to make. It asks us to stop multitasking, to release the need to perform, and to let go of the pressure to say something meaningful. It asks us to sit inside the not knowing, to let the awkward pause stretch, and to trust that silence is not absence but invitation.

This is not a skill we master once and for all. It is a posture we return to, again and again. Each moment becomes a doorway, inviting reflection. What is getting in the way right now? Is it my need to be useful? My discomfort with stillness? My desire to be somewhere else?

And when we notice it, gently and without shame, we set it aside. Not perfectly, and not every time, but with intention. In doing so, we begin to make space for someone else to unfold, for a deeper truth to surface, and for a kind of connection that does not need to impress, only to hold.

The next time someone speaks, notice the moment your mind reaches to jump in, to solve, to explain, to respond. Just notice it, and then wait. One breath longer than you usually would. That is all. One breath. Sometimes that single breath is the difference between being heard and being held, between being understood and being advised, between the kind of listening that fills space and the kind that opens it.

In that breath, something else may arrive. It might be quieter, truer, and undeniably real. A thread of connection strong enough to hold even the hardest things. And sometimes, that is enough.

Back to you

You can tell when someone is not really listening. They nod, smile, and say all the right things like *mm*, *yeah*, or *oh wow*, yet underneath, something is missing. They are not with you. They are waiting for their turn. Once you notice it, it is hard to unsee. It is like spotting the trick behind a magic show, when the sleight of hand becomes obvious even though the performance continues.

It happens constantly. You open up to someone, maybe after rehearsing the words in your head, or perhaps while fumbling your way toward a feeling you have not yet fully formed. There is a reason you are saying it, even if you cannot name it. But just as the thread begins to form, they cut in. You might say something like, *I don't know, I just woke up feeling off today, like I'm carrying something I can't quite name.* And before the thought even lands, they are already responding. *Ugh, I totally get that. I've been so burned out lately I could barely get out of bed this morning. Work is just nonstop...*

And just like that, the conversation turns to them.

That is what I call it now, sometimes even saying it aloud, gently and with a half-smile. *Back to you.* It is not meant to shame or scold, only to name what has happened. Some people do not notice and keep going. Others pause, realize, and apologize, maybe even inviting me to continue. By then, though, the moment is usually gone.

Listening is not about taking turns. It is not a tennis match of anecdotes. It is spacious and slow, offering someone the room to find their way not only to the words, but to the meaning beneath them. When we interrupt, even with something lighthearted or meant to connect, we do not just break the sentence. We interrupt the process. We stop something that is still becoming.

Research supports this. Psychologists have studied how interruptions affect connection, and the findings go deeper than simple awkwardness. A study in the *Journal of Language and Social Psychology* found that frequent interruptions, especially those that redirect focus, are linked to lower trust, reduced rapport, and a diminished sense of warmth. One experiment showed that people who were interrupted, even briefly, rated their conversation partners as less competent, less likable, and less safe.[7] Another study in the *Journal of Nonverbal Behavior* observed that men interrupted women significantly more often than the reverse, and not out of enthusiasm, but as a form of dismissal.[8]

Beyond the research, there is something more human at stake. When we interrupt, we do not just change the subject. We send a signal, subtle but sharp, that says our voice matters more than theirs in that moment. Over time, that message settles in. People stop trying to finish their thoughts. They begin editing themselves in advance, and sometimes they fold up mid-sentence.

I have felt this in friendships, in arguments, and in quiet, vulnerable moments. Someone begins to open the door to something raw or unresolved, and instead of stepping in with them, we pivot. We reroute the attention back to our own story, our own insight, our own need to be seen.

Sometimes it comes from nervousness. Sometimes it is care, mistranslated. We may genuinely believe that sharing our own version of pain is how we show empathy, and occasionally that is true. But more often it is not, it becomes a subtle hijack, a moment taken even with love, and it costs more than we realize. The speaker loses the chance to be heard. The listener loses the chance to truly witness. And the relationship loses a moment of depth that will not come back in quite the same way.

Through failing in more conversations than I can count, I have learned that one of the most powerful gifts I can offer is my full, quiet attention. Not my opinions or my story, and not even my insight, but simply space. It is harder than it sounds, because it requires discipline not to jump in, not to compare, and not to reach for relevance. But the reward is something that feels, at least to me, almost sacred.

Because when someone says what they truly mean, when they hear their own truth raw and unedited, perhaps for the first time, and you were the one who made space for that, it is not just a good conversation. It is a moment that can change people.

Chapter 4.

The science of listening

My marriage didn't collapse. It quieted.

It did not happen all at once, and it did not come with betrayal or raised voices. The change was slower, a quiet dimming shaped by a fatigue that ran deeper than sleep. It gathered in the background of early parenthood, with diapers, play groups, and sleepless nights, a life so full it began to press against the subtler things, the shared glances, the half-finished jokes, the small rituals that once tethered us beneath the noise.

Connection turned into something we postponed. I kept telling myself we would find time later, but later always slipped away. We still lived side by side, packing school lunches, brushing teeth, folding laundry, yet the space between us began to stretch. It was not conflict that widened it but silence, the kind that drifts in like fog, gentle yet disorienting, until even the most familiar ground feels subtly changed.

Junko grew quieter, not cold but further away. Conversations that once moved without effort now faltered, and her gaze no longer lingered. We stopped asking how the other was doing, not from neglect but from a quiet belief that the answer would no longer reach us. There was no rupture, only a slow drift.

On weekends I took the boys out for bike rides and camping trips, the same rituals I had loved in my own childhood. She turned toward her Japanese mothers' group, her community, a place where she did not need to explain herself in order to feel understood, a space where she could simply belong. I knew it made sense, yet it still hurt.

We were not fighting, yet we were no longer finding each other. It felt like two boats slowly drifting away from the same dock, not pushed by storm or blame but carried off by the steady pull of the current.

I was still trying. I went to marriage counselling on my own, hoping it might stir something, that if I could bring the right insight to the table it might reopen a door. But Junko had already begun to retreat inward. We remained good parents, steady and kind, yet the thread that once pulled us back to each other had begun to fray.

What I felt was not rage but grief, a quiet grief that settled behind the ribs, said little, and never left.

Not long after, I enrolled in a counselling course. Officially it was to build skills, perhaps even the beginning of a new career, but underneath it was a last attempt to believe that if I asked the right question or found the perfect phrase, I might still reach her. I did not. The course did not save the marriage, and there was

The science of listening

no cinematic moment of reconnection. What it gave me instead was something smaller and steadier, a way to let go without bitterness, to move through the ending with care, and to remain intact enough for our children, present and still whole.

The first thing I noticed during the course was how often I interrupted, not only out loud but inside my own mind. I was always preparing the next thought before the other person had finished theirs, listening for the gap I could fill or the mistake I could correct.

One instructor, soft-spoken and sharp-eyed, said something that lodged deep in me. She told us that the most healing thing you can do in conversation is not to speak, but to hold the silence long enough for the other person to feel safe inside it.

It did not come naturally. Silence made me restless, and I wanted to fix whatever was left unspoken. Still, I began to practice, first with classmates, then with clients, and eventually with Junko.

What I discovered, and what neuroscience now confirms, is that listening is not passive. It is not simply the absence of talking. It is something far more powerful, a form of co-regulation.

Rooted in polyvagal theory, developed by neuroscientist Stephen Porges, co-regulation describes how our nervous systems communicate and attune to one another in real time. When someone truly listens, not only with their ears but with their body, their breath, and their full attention, it carries a message. It tells the other person's system that they are safe. It eases tension and lowers the guard, not because of the words spoken but because of the way the moment is held.

Science supports this. Research on affective touch shows that simple, gentle contact communicates safety and empathy, serving as a powerful channel for human connection. Functional MRI studies further reveal that social support, including supportive touch, reduces the brain's threat response and softens the body's stress reactivity. At the heart of both findings is one essential experience, the felt sense of being accompanied and understood.[9]

When we feel heard, we settle, not only emotionally but also physiologically. From that settledness new things can emerge, including vulnerability, clarity, and change.

With Junko, I began to notice subtle shifts. We were still separating, yet the tone between us changed. I stopped interrupting and stopped offering fixes. Instead, I mirrored her words, not as a strategy but as an offering, a way of saying that I was still here. At times that was enough, not to save the marriage, but to let it end with grace and with dignity.

I remember one night at the dining table, as we sat sorting through logistics such as housing, parenting time, and how we would tell the boys. Panic rose in my chest along with the familiar urge to explain myself, to soften the edges, to make it better, yet this time I did not. I paused, I breathed, and I listened.

And in that stillness I heard not only her words but everything layered beneath them, grief, clarity, and, buried deeper still, a quiet hope that we might find a way through this with grace. I nodded and said, *wakarimasu*. I understand. And I did.

It did not solve anything in the practical sense, yet something shifted. The space between us softened. We remained intact, not only as co-parents but as two people still willing to meet each other with care.

That is the deeper shape of listening, not persuasion and not performance, but a steady presence that does not try to fix what is fragile and instead chooses to remain with it. Not every break can be mended, yet how we break matters, as does the way we carry one another through what follows.

The quiet power of presence

I remember the hush in the auditorium before he appeared, the low voices, the rustle of programs, a reverence that was not demanded but earned. We were waiting not only for a speaker but for something unspoken, something we could not quite name. I had come to see Eckhart Tolle with questions, not from doubt, but because his book *The Power of Now* had stirred something in me. I did not know if the stillness I felt in those pages was real or simply the pull of good writing.

When he stepped onto the stage there was no attempt at performance, no dramatic pause, no soaring cadence, only a man in simple clothes walking calmly, as if time did not pull at him the way it pulls at the rest of us. He sat, looked around, and remained silent for a long minute, a silence so sustained it stopped feeling like absence and began to take on its own presence. The air grew dense, not with tension but with stillness, with something softly alive.

Something shifted in me, or perhaps in the room. It was not a spectacle, it felt cellular. The silence was not empty but inhabited by grounded attention and unforced calm, a stillness that did not erase expectation but quietly transformed it. He did not seem aloof or detached, only available, unpressured, unperforming, entirely here. And it struck me.

It reminded me of the dojo, of those rare moments when movement became a form of listening, when my training partner and I moved without force or strategy, simply attuned. One rhythm, one breath, no edges.

That evening gave me no tools, no framework, no three-step path. It left me with something quieter and more unsettling, a question. What if the most powerful thing I can offer in any moment is not insight, or skill, or even compassion, but being? Not the kind of being that waits to speak, holds a posture, or scripts an answer, but the kind that allows itself to be altered by what it encounters.

The science of listening

Tolle did not teach that through words. He embodied it. And in that embodiment, something in me recognized a destination I had been moving toward without knowing it. Being is not passive. It does not need volume to carry weight, and it does not require direction to be meaningful. It is power, quiet but not small, soft but not weak, the kind that moves inward, into the silent interior spaces where change begins without force and transformation arrives without announcement. Perhaps that is the kind of power that endures.

After Junko and I separated, something shifted. The routines stayed the same, with school runs, teeth brushing, and wrestling on the couch, and life kept moving. Yet beneath the surface there was a subtle tightness in the air, a kind of static that lingers when something essential has changed shape and no one quite knows how to name it.

At bedtime my youngest would sometimes whisper, thin as tissue, if he could sleep at Mum's. Even wrapped in his own blanket, surrounded by toys and the warm glow of his lamp, he would say it with a delicacy that cut through me, *I want to sleep at Mum's*. He did not ask every night, but when he did a small part of me cracked, quietly and invisibly. I nodded, sometimes smiled, and helped him gather what he needed before taking him back. It was not defiance but truth. Her house had been his only home, and however gently we had introduced the change, it still felt like a tear in the fabric.

My eldest carried it differently. He laughed at my jokes, came on bike rides, played along. Yet every so often, when he didn't know I was watching, I would catch a flicker, a moment of quiet mapping, as if he were trying to chart the contours of this new life. There were no breakdowns, no blowups, only questions hanging in the space between words. They were not unraveling, but they were carrying it. And so was I.

I kept trying to soften it, telling them it was going to be okay, that Mum was just down the road, that nothing was really changing. I meant every word, yet their shoulders stayed tense, their breath stayed shallow, and their eyes kept searching the room for something that felt solid. Then something in my body, shaped by the mat and by practice, told me to stop talking.

So I did. I tried something else. I sat beside them on the edge of the bed, matched their breath, and let the silence stretch without rushing to fill it. Sometimes I rested a hand on their back, not to fix or steer but simply to stay, to say I am here. Their breathing slowed, the tension in their bodies began to ease. Not because I had found the right words, but because I had not tried to use any at all.

I didn't know the term co-regulation then, but I knew the shape of it, and now I was witnessing it, quiet, powerful, unmistakable. It was not an explanation, not comfort, but presence. I began to notice how often I had spoken when silence would have served better, how often I had reached for words when what was needed was simply

The science of listening

staying. And it was not only with my kids, but with friends, colleagues, even strangers.

Being listened to, truly listened to, is rarer than we imagine. It does not always sound like anything. Sometimes it is a hand that does not pull away, a breath that stays steady while another falters, a gaze that holds without trying to manage. Listening begins long before language. It begins with safety, and safety begins in the body. Sometimes that means letting someone falter without stepping in, or staying still while they unravel. Not fixing, not interpreting, just staying.

It is silence that is not awkward or absent but held, spacious, grounded, unflinching. A quiet that carries the message that you do not have to be anything else right now. The nervous system hears it, feels it, and begins to trust it. In a world that rushes to respond, to advise, to perform, this kind of listening is more than gentle. It is radical.

Late one afternoon, in a room so still it made the silence feel almost audible, a man named Jim sat across from his therapist. Light pooled softly in the corners, and everything in the space seemed designed to be non-intrusive, to step quietly out of the way. Jim sat rigid in the armchair, his hands knotted in his lap and his shoulders drawn inward, not in collapse but in resistance, as though holding something in place that had been pressing upward for weeks, perhaps longer.

He had been coming to these sessions for more than a month, each one a slow, careful orbit around something unnamed. He spoke of stress, long hours, the way his wife seemed to look through him. His stories came in fragments, as if he were laying down puzzle pieces without revealing the picture. But today felt different. The way he sat carried a heavier stillness, not the peaceful kind but the kind that holds its breath. Whatever he had been circling was now close enough to touch, too present to avoid, and still too raw to name.

Dr. Thompson did not press. He didn't lean in, tilt his head, or fill the space with coaxing questions. He simply remained, present, open, steady. His stillness was not passive but carried its own gravity. He held the room the way a shoreline holds the tide, not controlling it, not chasing it, simply available when it was ready to meet him.

Eventually Jim spoke, his voice low and hesitant, thick with the weight of someone unsure if he was allowed to say the truth out loud. He said that he had spoken words to his wife he should not have, that he was angry and did not stop himself.

He paused, his eyes falling to the floor and his body tightening again as if bracing for judgment. He expected correction, analysis, some subtle flicker of disapproval, but none came.

Dr. Thompson nodded, his tone calm and grounded.

The science of listening

"Thank you for telling me," he said. "That took courage."

There was no dissection, no reframing, no rush to explain. Only acceptance. In that small, seemingly simple gesture, something in Jim unlatched. He exhaled, not in relief exactly, but with permission. For the first time in weeks, he was no longer alone inside the weight he carried. He did not have to prove anything or perform regret. He could simply be what he was, someone who had done harm and was still worthy of being met.

That kind of listening, quiet and unconditional, is at the heart of what Carl Rogers called unconditional positive regard. It is a presence that does not require anyone to justify their pain. It carries a wordless signal that you can stop holding your breath now. Rogers once wrote that when a person is hurting, confused, troubled, anxious, alienated, or terrified, the gentle and sensitive companionship of an empathic stance can bring illumination and healing. Dr. Thompson was not offering insight or digging for answers. He was doing something harder, staying with steadiness, with care, without retreat.

That steadiness made space for Jim to continue, not only with the facts of what happened but with the deeper currents beneath them, fear, shame, and the loneliness of not knowing how to be heard or how to hear someone else. What began as a confession became clarity, not because anything had been solved but because something had been held.

Decades after Rogers, research confirmed what therapists like Dr. Thompson had long known. A major meta-analysis in psychotherapy found that the quality of the relationship, including the therapist's empathy, congruence, and acceptance, mattered more than any specific technique. Healing was not primarily about tools but about trust.[10]

And this truth reaches far beyond therapy rooms. In daily life, in living rooms and lunch breaks, in text threads and hospital visits, what matters most is often not what we say but that we stay. That we do not flinch when the hard things arrive. That we resist the urge to wrap someone's pain in a tidy insight just so we can move on feeling helpful.

To sit with someone in their uncertainty, to say with our presence that they do not have to be perfect to be heard, is one of the most profound gifts we can give. Jim left the session lighter. The conflict at home was still unresolved, yet the shame no longer gripped him in the same way. He was no longer scrambling to outrun it. He was beginning to understand it.

Real change does not begin with answers but with safety, and safety begins with being met exactly as we are.

Learning to listen to what's not being said

When I first enrolled in the counselling course, I imagined it might lead to a new career. I pictured a quiet room, a soft voice, a grounded presence helping others untangle what had knotted inside them. It felt like a natural step, an extension of my curiosity about human behavior, and perhaps a lifeline as well, something steady to hold while my own life was beginning to fray at the edges.

It didn't take long to realize I wasn't chasing a profession. I was searching for a way of being. What drew me in was not the role of counsellor but the listening, the kind that doesn't reach to steer or soothe but simply stays, the kind that does not shrink from silence or mistake quiet for absence. I was not looking for answers. I was looking for an attentive stillness, one that does not perform, persuade, or push.

The course, and later my deeper studies in Cognitive Behavioural Therapy (CBT), offered that, not clarity through easy fixes but a way in, a framework for listening that did not depend on mastery or charisma but on a discipline of attention, of breath, of embodied awareness.

CBT is often introduced through tools such as identifying cognitive distortions, mapping belief systems, and challenging automatic thoughts. Those tools matter, and they work, yet beneath them lies something older and more essential. What we hear shapes how we feel, and how we listen shapes what others are willing to reveal.

In our role-play sessions we would sit across from a partner and listen as they spoke about something painful. Our task was not to respond or interpret but to reflect, to stay close to the emotion beneath the story, to follow its contours gently, and to offer back what we heard. The aim was not to be insightful but to be accurate, attentive, and receptive.

I remember one exercise vividly. My partner spoke about the weight of parenting, the kind of overwhelm that grows not from a single crisis but from the slow accumulation of invisible tasks and unspoken expectations. I could see it in the sag of their shoulders and hear it in the catch of their breath. Everything in me wanted to normalize it, to reassure them, to share a story of my own, yet I did not. I stayed with them and let the silence breathe.

Then I said, "It sounds like you feel as if you are carrying all of it alone." They paused, their eyes welled, and something in them softened.

That was the moment I understood what Carl Rogers meant when he wrote that when someone really hears you without passing judgment or trying to mold you, it feels damn good. He believed healing does not begin with strategy but with safety, the kind of safety that allows you to stop defending, stop impressing, and stop translating your pain into something more palatable just to be received.

That idea reshaped how I offered support, not as solutions but as presence, not as performance but as offering. Later, when I encountered the neuroscience behind these moments, it confirmed what Rogers had known intuitively, that being truly heard changes us, not only metaphorically but physiologically. The nervous system calms, the heart rate slows, and the brain begins to trust again. From that trust, vulnerability becomes possible.

It left me wondering how many conversations in my life had been shaped not by what was said but by whether the other person felt safe enough to speak at all. That question stayed with me and began to change how I listened to my children, my friends, and my colleagues. I noticed how often I filled silences, even with good intentions, how quickly I moved toward problem-solving when someone simply needed to be witnessed, and how my impulse to help sometimes crowded out a quieter need to be seen.

But the most lasting shift was inward.

CBT, for all its focus on cognitive patterns and behavioral loops, is not only about understanding others. It teaches you to listen to yourself, to notice the commentary running beneath your choices, the beliefs you did not realize you had inherited, and the judgments you cast before a sentence is even finished.

I began to ask myself the same questions I was trained to ask others. *What is really happening here? What emotion is underneath this reaction? What story am I believing right now, and is it actually true?*

That shift from reacting to reflecting did not make me immune to missteps, but it made me slower to rush, softer in my assessments, and more curious in the face of discomfort. It did not make me perfect. It made me more available, more porous, and more willing to stay.

Listening, I have come to believe, is not only a technique or a skill but a posture, a discipline of presence in a world that constantly pulls us toward distraction, urgency, and performance. And although I never became a counsellor in the formal sense, those years gave me something deeper. They taught me how to hold space, to let things remain unclear, and to hear what is not said. In doing so, they gave me back my attention, and with it a different way of moving through the world.

Closing the distance

If I have learned anything over these years, through the slow unraveling of a marriage, the raw intimacy of parenting, the quiet rigor of study, and the humbling practice of martial arts, it is that we are all aching to be

The science of listening

understood. Yet most of us were never truly taught how to understand in the way that matters. We learned how to speak, how to argue, and how to present ourselves with clarity and conviction. But to sit beside someone without defense or distraction, to receive them just as they are, is a different kind of knowledge entirely.

Today's world does not reward that kind of listening. It rewards volume, speed, and certainty. It celebrates the quick take, the confident stance, the sharpened edge. In a culture moving this fast, there is little room for nuance, for the slow reveal, for the quieter truths that take time to emerge.

In a culture moving at this pace, it becomes easy to mistake noise for connection and to confuse a flurry of responses with conversation. We begin to believe our worth lies in how swiftly we reply or how firmly we position ourselves, rather than in how deeply we listen.

Beneath all that posturing, behind the curated feeds, the polished opinions, and the impulse to impress, something softer remains, a hunger. Not for more content or certainty, but for something slower and more real, for attention that does not need to be right, for empathy that does not reach to fix, for the rare relief of being heard without interruption or reinterpretation. Simply received, as we are.

That hunger shows up everywhere, in our relationships, in our parenting, in the way we lead, and in how we meet ourselves. When it goes unmet, something essential begins to fray. We speak past each other, defend instead of listen, soothe what has not been named, and perform instead of connect.

It does not have to stay that way. Both research and lived experience point to the same truth, that when we feel truly heard, we feel safer. Our breath deepens, our nervous system relaxes, and we let down our guard, not because someone has fixed us but because we no longer have to brace ourselves to be misunderstood.

That is not sentiment, it is biology. And when we learn to offer that kind of listening, not only to the story but to the ache beneath it, something in the room begins to shift. The atmosphere changes, and the emotional distance starts to close. Not perfectly, not without effort or mess, but enough.

Enough for someone to feel less alone in what they carry. Enough to ease the grip of shame or fear. Enough to remind us that healing rarely begins with the perfect response. It begins with the quiet and steady act of staying.

This first part of the book has been about the noise, the habits, systems, distractions, and quiet fears that pull us away from each other and from ourselves. It has looked at the ways we interrupt, retreat, and over-explain, and at the cultural currents that prize speaking over hearing and certainty over attention.

The science of listening

But naming the problem is only the beginning. Real change does not come from understanding listening as a concept, or from reading the right words, or memorizing the right terms. It comes through practice, by returning again and again to the places where listening matters most.

Not in grand gestures but in the quiet, unspectacular moments of daily life. It shows itself in the pause before we reply, in the breath we take instead of defending ourselves, in the choice to stay present when it would be easier to retreat, scroll, or shut down. In those small decisions, something shifts.

We begin to listen not because we are supposed to, but because something in us remembers why it matters. Not perfectly and not for praise, but with care.

That is where we are heading next, into the lived spaces where listening takes shape, into families, conflict, intimacy, leadership, and the quiet, ongoing conversation we carry within ourselves.

There will be no scripts and no tidy conclusions. Only an invitation to show up differently, with more curiosity, more steadiness, and a greater willingness to let silence speak, to let discomfort teach, and to let listening become less a skill and more a way of moving through the world.

Part II: Practice

Chapter 5.

The art of listening

Advancing through the kyu grades in Aikido is like walking deeper into a forest. At the edge everything is bright and open, the path clearly marked and the movements carefully mapped. You learn to fall without fear and to stand with quiet intention. You hold a bokken as if it carries real weight, practising until each gesture settles into your body. There is comfort in this choreography, a rhythm to every step forward, and with each knot in your belt you make a simple declaration that you are present and that you belong.

As you move towards your black belt grading, the forest begins to change. The techniques are still present, yet the atmosphere shifts and something in the air feels different. The space between movements becomes vivid, and timing, breath, and the shape of your attention start to matter in ways they did not before. It is no longer only about motion but about attunement, and you are invited to listen in a new way, not with your ears but with your entire nervous system.

I remember those years clearly, training several nights a week and again on Sunday mornings, walking home sore and exhausted with bruises I could never explain to anyone outside the dojo. It was not about injury but about imprint, the kind of lesson that is absorbed in the body long before the mind can name it.

The dojo was no longer only a place to train but a mirror and a threshold, a space where I met myself in full. I encountered not just the parts that moved with ease but also the parts that resisted, the ones that held tension and had not yet learned how to yield.

Sensei spoke often but never casually, and his words always carried weight. At times he would stop the class mid-movement to unpack a principle, moving with ease between the technical and the philosophical. It was never only about how to pivot but also about why, never only about the shape but also about the source. His words landed like stones in still water, small and deliberate yet rippling far beyond their size.

Occasionally, when something began to click and a movement was not perfect but carried the right intent, he would simply say, "That'll grow." It was less praise than recognition, an acknowledgment that something had taken root even if it had not yet fully bloomed. Because he did not give compliments freely, what he said stayed with you, and when he said them, you felt them.

At the end of each class we sat in a circle in *seiza*, our knees often touching the students beside us. One by one we had the chance to speak, offering what we noticed, where we struggled, and what we were beginning to see, not only in the technique but in ourselves. The circle was never about performance, it was a space to stay with each

The art of listening

other's reflections and to witness them without rushing to respond, reframe, or fold them into our own story.

One person might speak about the tension in their hips while another spoke of grief, and sometimes the stories had little to do with Aikido yet everything to do with life. Still, the mat held it all.

More than martial arts, we were learning how to listen. Not the kind that nods politely while waiting to speak or searches for an opening, but the kind that slows the breath and lingers in silence long enough for something to be revealed. It was the kind of listening that resists the urge to move simply to fill the space.

That circle changed how I understood communication, not as the skill of speaking well but as the discipline of remaining open long enough to fully receive what another person is offering, without rushing to shape it or resolve it.

Around that time Sensei mentioned a book, *The 7 Habits of Highly Effective People*. He did not explain or elaborate, only said, "Read it," as if it were part of the training. There was no pitch and no context, just a simple directive left in the stillness after class.

I did not know it then, but Habit Five, *Seek first to understand, then to be understood,* would become a guiding thread for years to come. It was never a strategy but a rhythm I later recognised in the teachings of Marshall Rosenberg, the founder of Nonviolent Communication. Behind every expression lies a feeling, and beneath that feeling, a need. Language suddenly gave shape to what I had already felt in my bones.

One teacher showed me how to move, another taught me how to feel, and a third taught me how to stay. Through their different languages they offered the same invitation, which was to listen not passively but with my whole being, to release control and performance, and to trust that real, grounded, unguarded connection is enough.

That is where true connection begins, not in words but in the space we are willing to create for someone else to arrive fully and without apology. Within that space something rare becomes possible, not only communication but recognition.

As I moved closer to black belt the techniques began to fade into the background. I still practised them endlessly, with rolls, pins, and footwork drills etched so deeply into my body that I could perform them half-asleep. Yet what held my attention was no longer the movements themselves but the quality of how they were done, how my way of being shaped the energy on the mat, and how the awareness of others in turn shaped me.

Some nights I partnered with someone whose grip was tight, whose movements were hurried, and whose rhythm was slightly out of sync, and I felt it immediately.

The art of listening

Their tension became mine, my breath would catch, my centre would rise, and in an instant we were no longer training together but negotiating control. It was not a fight but a quiet friction, one I already knew well outside the dojo.

If I softened instead by widening my stance, deepening my breath, and moving with their rhythm rather than resisting, things began to shift. They softened as well, and the technique flowed between us, not imposed but exchanged, a current rather than a contest.

I did not yet have the language for it, but I was living what it meant to co-regulate. It was an embodied reciprocity that moved breath to breath, posture to posture, and tone to tone. I was not only learning how to take someone's balance but also how to create it with them.

Outside the dojo the same patterns appeared. In conversations and meetings I noticed how often people were not truly listening but simply waiting for a gap, holding their place until it was their turn to speak. I saw how often I had done the same, mistaking quickness for care and rushing to fill the space before someone had fully arrived in it.

On the mat that approach never worked, because you had to wait, to feel, to sense, and to respond rather than react. I began to wonder how things might change if that kind of listening were carried into every part of life.

Rosenberg's work gave me the language for what I had long sensed. Feelings arise from needs, even when they're buried beneath layers of expression. It was not a technique but a lens. Covey's Habit Five carried the same clarity and urged me to seek first to understand. Not to agree, not to respond, not to fix, but simply to understand.

In the circle at the end of class that principle came alive. No one interrupted or corrected. There was no applause and no advice, only space. Over time that space began to feel sacred. What we were practising was not passive attention but a kind of active stillness, a discipline of staying open, resisting the urge to insert yourself, and meeting someone's truth without turning it into your own.

Most of the time we simply listened, and at times Sensei would speak, not to instruct but to reflect, offering a question, a mirror, or a thread of insight with no weight and no expectation. His words never sought to redirect, only to deepen, and in that way the circle became the dojo within the dojo. The real training was found not only in how well we moved but also in how deeply we paid attention.

When I prepared for my black belt I realised the test was not really physical. It asked for steadiness under pressure, awareness in motion, and the ability to stay connected to both my partner and myself, on and off the mat. The techniques still mattered, yet what mattered more was who I had become through them and who I was still becoming.

The art of listening

Letting go of control

There is a moment in every real conversation, sometimes early and sometimes just before it ends, when something inside begins to loosen. You stop gripping the reins, stop composing your reply, and stop scanning for signs that you have been heard. Instead you listen, not passively or from a distance, but with humility and the quiet strength it takes to release control and lean, however gently, into trust.

When that happens the rhythm of the conversation changes. The current slows, the tension that was once tightly wound begins to ease, and what was guarded starts to surface, not with drama but with depth. I did not learn this in a workshop or through sudden insight. It arrived quietly in an ordinary conversation with a friend.

She had just launched a business, something built slowly with heart and conviction, yet it was not going well. Revenue had stalled, pressure was mounting, and a relationship she deeply valued had begun to fray. She was carrying too much, holding it with the brittle kind of grace that looks like composure from the outside but feels dangerously close to collapse from within.

As she spoke I felt my reflexes stir, the part of me that wanted to offer something, anything. A business idea, a reframe, a book she had not yet read. The scaffolding of a response began to assemble itself in my mind, piece by eager piece, yet there was something in her voice, raw and unguarded, that made me pause.

She was not asking for insight but for space, so I stayed quiet. I nodded and listened, not as a strategy but as a choice. She kept going and then stopped, the silence stretching between us, and I let it. That was when her body shifted. Her jaw softened and she exhaled fully, as if she had been waiting for permission to let go.

"Thanks," she said quietly. "You're the only one who just listens. Everyone else tries to fix it."

It was not a compliment but a kind of relief, a sign that something had begun to uncoil. It happened not because I solved anything but because she no longer had to carry it alone.

That moment stayed with me, not for what I said but for the fact that I finally stopped trying to say the right thing.

Long before I encountered the research I saw it in my own life. When people feel safe, their bodies respond, and neuroscience confirms the same. Studies show that when trust and social support are present, oxytocin increases, cortisol decreases, and the body's stress response eases. In that softening a different kind of conversation becomes possible, one that is not centred on resolution but on release.[11]

This applies not only in intimate relationships but everywhere. In organisations, trust-based leaders who listen without reflexively correcting or redirecting create

The art of listening

more resilient teams. They are not less decisive, only more attentive, and that attentiveness signals that this is a place where truth can land without the need for armour.

I saw this most clearly with my children. When one of them was upset my instinct was to explain, to reassure, or to search for the perfect words that might make it better. Yet more often what they needed was not explanation but space, not silence as absence but silence as offering, a ground on which something real could finally land.

The hardest part was trusting that this was enough. Control often wears the mask of care, advice can feel like help, and jumping in can feel like love. Yet when these instincts are overused they crowd out the very thing we are trying to invite, closing the door before the real story has even been told.

Marshall Rosenberg wrote that most of what we say, especially when we are hurting, is only the surface. Beneath that surface lies a feeling, and beneath that feeling lies a need. To reach it, someone has to listen, not to interpret or fix but simply to witness. That kind of listening begins with trust in the other person's process, trust in silence, and trust that being fully with someone is sometimes enough.

It is easy to forget this in a world that rewards speed and spectacle. The loudest voice wins online, and the fastest thinker commands the room. Even in parenting we are taught that having an answer is the same as having authority. Those patterns do not build connection, they build performance. At best they produce compliance, and at worst they create resistance.

Letting go of control does not mean disappearing or withholding care. It means creating steady and grounded space for someone else to find their own way, listening with your whole body, showing up with your breath, your pauses, and your willingness to stay with what feels uncomfortable. It also means trusting that when someone feels safe the deeper truth will come forward, not because we led them there but because we did not get in the way. This is not simply a technique but a way of being, the place where real connection begins.

One moment that has stayed with me did not happen in a workshop or on the mat but in a conversation with my brother, a time when I did not listen the way I wish I had.

We are close now and have been for years, but growing up our relationship was often tense, filled with the everyday friction that feels outsized when you are young and still trying to define your edges. Around the time I turned seventeen and he was twenty, something shifted between us. The arguments gave way to long conversations, trips away, and shared albums passed back and forth like offerings. Without ever naming it we began to trust each other, and a quiet loyalty took shape, unspoken yet deeply felt.

The art of listening

Then came Melbourne's long and disorienting lockdowns. My eldest son had just started high school and, with an earnest curiosity that felt rare and precious, had chosen the trumpet as his instrument. Before we could borrow one from the school the lockdown began, and I remembered that my brother had Dad's old trumpet stored somewhere at his place. It seemed like a simple solution, just a practical request.

I called him and asked politely if we could borrow it for a few weeks until school reopened. He said no, flatly and without hesitation. There was no explanation, only a firm refusal.

I was stunned. It was not for me but for his nephew, for school, for something small and necessary in an already difficult year. I replayed my tone, wondering if I had overstepped somehow, but I could not find the flaw. In the gap between what I expected and what I received, something old and sharp rose in me. Instead of pausing and being curious I let the reflex win. I let my frustration choose the words, and they landed harder than they should have.

He did not respond. There was no fight, no unpacking, no resolution. Only silence.

Even now I am not sure what was happening for him. It may have been about Dad, about memory and attachment and not wanting to let go. It may have been something in my voice that came across more like a demand than a request. Or perhaps it had nothing to do with me at all, and he was carrying something I never thought to ask about.

What I do know is that I was not really listening. I heard his refusal and built an entire story around it, one that cast me as the reasonable one and him as the withholding one. It was a story shaped by my hurt, coloured by assumption, and driven by the need to feel justified.

The thing we do not often admit about listening is that it is not only about attention but also about interpretation, and that process begins long before the other person speaks. It begins with the filter we are listening through. In that moment my filter was thick with disappointment. I did not hear uncertainty, or sentimentality, or even boundaries. I heard rejection.

It is easy to fall into this, especially with someone close to us. The moment their response does not match the shape we were hoping for, we stop listening. We fill the gaps with our own meaning and turn a simple "no" into a moral failing. Yet the way we listen profoundly shapes what we hear.

When we listen with openness we begin to notice things we might otherwise miss. We hear the hesitation in someone's voice, the breath they hold before answering, and the way their silence feels less like distance and more like protection. When we listen through the lens of being wronged we find insult where there is only uncertainty, and we interpret hesitation as rejection and quietness as disconnection.

Real listening means stepping back from assumptions and making space not only for what is being said but also for the possibility that we do not yet understand the full story. Sometimes that is the most honest kind of empathy we can offer, not agreement or resolution but the willingness to hear more than our own version.

How we shape what we hear

In 1990, a Stanford graduate student named Elizabeth Newton conducted the "tappers and listeners" experiment. Participants tapped out familiar songs on a table, expecting listeners to identify them about half the time. In reality, listeners guessed correctly only 2.5% of the time, just 3 out of 120 attempts, even though tappers had assumed a 50% success rate.[12]

The gap came from a simple truth. The tappers carried the melody in their heads while the listeners did not. They heard the same rhythm but experienced something entirely different. It is a deceptively simple experiment with profound implications. We do not just hear, we interpret, and we fill in the gaps based on what we expect rather than on what is actually there.

Psychologists call this "top-down processing," a filter shaped by memory, emotion, and belief. When we listen only to confirm what we already think we bend the truth into our own shape. When we listen to understand we remain open, even to perspectives that feel unfamiliar or uncomfortable.

I have felt this viscerally on the mat. In Aikido the way you receive an attack, the way you listen to your partner's energy, shapes everything. If you meet force with force you lock into resistance, but if you soften your stance, slow your breath, and move with them rather than react, something shifts. Flow replaces friction. The technique may remain the same, yet the intention changes, and with it the outcome.

In real conversation it is no different, because listening through defensiveness distorts what is said and listening from a place of control constricts it. When we listen instead with genuine curiosity and openness, we create the space for someone to unfold freely, without the need to perform or prove anything, but simply to be.

Neuroscience supports this. fMRI studies show that when we anticipate conflict the amygdala, the brain's alarm system, becomes active. Our focus narrows, we brace, and we lose the ability to hear nuance. When we feel safe the medial prefrontal cortex engages, the part of the brain connected with empathy, integration, and trust. That is when real listening becomes possible, not only to the words themselves but to the human being beneath them.[18]

This is why the very same remark can either wound or resonate depending on how it is received. When listeners sense judgment they close, and when they feel care they open. The words may be identical, yet the quality of listening changes everything.

When we learn to listen for what is not said, the emotion, the longing, or the fear beneath anger, we begin to translate the hidden layer. Frustration can be heard not as defiance but as confusion, anger not as aggression but as grief, and sarcasm not as dismissal but as distance. In this way we stop reacting to noise and begin responding to need.

This is not magic. It is attention, a discipline, a moment-by-moment commitment to listening, breath by breath and conversation by conversation. How we listen shapes more than what we hear, it shapes the space between us. It determines whether tension becomes a battleground or a bridge, whether we retreat into certainty or lean into connection. And perhaps most importantly, the way we listen to others becomes the blueprint for how we listen to ourselves.

The edge of listening

If martial arts has taught me anything it is that every meaningful practice lives at an edge, the place where your habits meet something unfamiliar, uncomfortable, and alive. Listening is no different.

There is the kind of listening that comes easily, when the other person is calm, the stakes are low, and there is mutual respect with space to breathe. That kind of listening nourishes trust and builds connection, yet it is not where transformation lives. Growth begins where listening becomes difficult.

I remember one conversation early in a relationship, a quiet evening that turned unexpectedly tense. We had begun with something mundane and practical, yet somewhere along the way her responses started to land sideways. A simple suggestion felt loaded, and a gentle disagreement registered as criticism. It was as if I were speaking into a mirror that subtly warped every word I said.

Frustration rose before I could catch it, carried by the sharp and involuntary urge to defend myself. I wanted to clarify, to correct, to explain my intention and close the gap between what I meant and what she heard. Yet something held me back. This was the edge, not because I had done something wrong but because I was being asked to stay steady in the space between us without demanding to be understood. I needed to resist the pull to rescue my image and remain grounded even as her defensiveness began to stir my own.

So I stayed quiet, not in withdrawal but with grounded curiosity. I listened not only to the words she spoke but also to the ache beneath them, a layer shaped by our exchange as well as by her history, her fears, and the meanings that lived beyond language. It did not resolve everything, yet the charge dissipated. The air between us shifted and in that change I realised that listening does not always begin with mutual understanding. Sometimes

The art of listening

it begins with the willingness to stay, even when understanding feels out of reach.

This is what I have come to call the edge of listening, the moment when emotions run high, judgment tightens, and your footing begins to slip while the old reflexes call you to retreat, react, shut down, or push through. It is also the moment that carries the most potential.

On the mat we train for this every day, not to overpower but to remain soft under pressure, to meet force without collapsing, and to stay open even while in motion. Gradually something shifts, not only in the body but in the nervous system. The flinch begins to fade and trust in the space takes its place. With time you learn that the edge is not the place where you fail but the place where you grow.

Carl Rogers once wrote that the great majority of us cannot listen, because we feel compelled to evaluate, and listening itself feels too dangerous. He said the first requirement is courage. That is what this edge asks of us, not mastery and not poise but courage. It is the courage to stay open when every instinct wants to close, to remain curious even when you are certain you are right, to hear what is hard without rushing to fix it, and to let discomfort deepen the connection rather than derail it.

Neuroscience echoes this truth. Studies show that when we meet emotional intensity with calm attention and regulate instead of react, the amygdala quiets and the prefrontal cortex becomes active. In that shift, the body steadies and the mind opens, making genuine connection more possible. Through steady attention we do not just feel calmer together, we begin to co-regulate.[14]

So perhaps the edge we fear most, the raw and reactive space that feels unresolved, is not something to escape but the very place where we come alive. It is never perfect and never without effort, yet it brings us into life more fully. Each time we meet that edge and remain, something within us expands, and over time we become someone others can trust. It is not because we always agree but because we have learned to listen, especially when it is hard.

Chapter 6.

Different ways of listening

It often begins with a phrase like "I'm fine." Sometimes it's "Sure," or "It's all good," or "Whatever you want." These words seem generous and easy, agreeable on the surface, but if you listen closely, you can feel the tension beneath them. A pause lingers a little too long. There's a flicker behind the eyes, a jaw held tight in a way that doesn't quite match the words. The conversation moves on, but something in the body stays behind.

I didn't always hear it. In my early twenties, as I stepped into my first serious relationships, I took those words at face value. I believed I was being respectful by trusting what she said. If she told me it was okay to go out, to rehearse with the boys, to make plans, I accepted it. I'd kiss her goodbye, guitar slung over my shoulder, and leave feeling reassured. She said it was fine. What else was I supposed to do?

But the silence that followed never felt peaceful. There were no explosions, no slammed doors. Only a slow, steady drift. Her tone cooled, her touch grew more distant, and the space between us widened in quiet, icy ways. When I asked what was wrong, she would look at me and say, "Nothing. I told you it was fine."

Technically, she had. But something in me sensed otherwise. I had felt it in the hesitation, in the way the words landed slightly off, yet I didn't trust myself to name what I heard. I hadn't yet learned to listen for the signal beneath the sentence.

Most of us are never taught that kind of listening, especially not as men. We are raised to track the literal, to follow rules, interpret logic, and wait for clear requests. Yet relationships do not live in logic. They live in tone and timing, in the quiet music that moves beneath the words.

Now, when my partner says "That's fine," I tune in not only to her words but to her whole presence. I notice the shift in her breath, the way her gaze drifts and then returns, the small clench in her shoulders. These moments are not mysteries, they are messages. At times I name what I sense, gently and with care, and I might say with a smile that softens the edge, "That sounded like a three-out-of-ten fine. Do you want to tell me what's really going on?"

It is not an interrogation but an invitation, a way of saying that I see you, not only in the words you speak but in what you are holding back, and that I would rather meet the truth than drift along in the comfort of pretending. More often than not, that invitation opens something, a breath, a sigh, sometimes an eye-roll, and then words spoken more softly. She might say, "I just wish we had talked about it first." Or, "I feel a bit left out."

Different ways of listening

Or, "I had a rough day and was hoping we would spend the evening together." These are things I never would have known if I had only listened with my ears.

This kind of listening asks more of us. It requires stillness, curiosity, and the courage to hold the pause between what is said and what is meant, without rushing to close it. Most of us have learned to say "I'm fine" when we are not, often out of fatigue or fear. We learn not to be difficult or needy or dramatic, and somewhere along the way we absorb the message that honesty can cost us. So we soften our truth, wrap it in politeness, and hope quietly that someone will notice what was left unsaid.

When no one does, something breaks. It is not loud, but a small fracture in trust, a subtle feeling of being unseen, of sending a signal and watching it drift through the room unanswered.

I have come to think of it like tuning a radio. You cannot force the signal, only listen through the static for the tremor in the breath, the catch in the voice, the gap between the words and the body that delivers them. At first it all sounds like noise, but if you stay with it, and care enough to wait, something begins to come through.

The "I'm fine" that means "I'm overwhelmed." The "Whatever you want" that means "I don't feel considered." The silence that means "Please, don't go."

What I didn't yet understand was that this same pattern would show up differently in my next relationship. Not in what she left unsaid, but in what I refused to let her say her own way.

Learning to listen with more than ears

My son was twelve when he sat the entrance exam for the Select Entry Accelerated Learning program, SEAL for short. We had gone over everything, the format, the strategies, the pacing, and on paper he was ready. Yet that morning, something in the air felt different.

We moved through our usual routine of getting ready for school, but his movements slowed and his words grew sparse. It was not the focused quiet I sometimes saw in him before a challenge. This quiet felt brittle, as though it were holding its breath and waiting for something unnamed to pass. His shoulders edged upward, his chest stiffened, and his gaze darted across the room as if searching for an exit, not from the building but from the pressure gathering inside.

Then, in the middle of the hallway, he stopped. His hands hung mid-motion and his eyes grew distant, his whole body caught in a pause that seemed to speak everything he could not. He was not simply preparing for a test, he was overwhelmed.

I asked how he was feeling. "I'm okay," he said, but his voice and body told a different story. His jaw was set, his breathing shallow, and I could feel the charge in the air, tight and coiled, waiting. He was not afraid of the

Different ways of listening

questions on the page, he was afraid of what they might mean, of what failure might say about him, and of what it might say to me.

I could have brushed past it, telling him to take a breath and simply do his best, but something in me paused. What he needed was not logic or strategy but contact.

So I knelt beside him, not looming and not fixing, simply near. We were eye to eye and breath to breath. I didn't say, "You'll be fine," because I didn't know that, and I didn't say, "Don't be scared," because it was clear he was. What I could offer was myself, steady and quiet, with the kind of attention that asks for nothing in return.

"Let's breathe together," I said.

He looked at me with uncertainty, then nodded, and so we did. In the hush of the hallway we breathed together, in through the nose and out again, slow and steady until the ground returned beneath us. I didn't explain what I was doing. I simply let him borrow my rhythm until he found his own.

At first nothing changed. Then gradually his shoulders softened, his breathing evened out, and his eyes met mine again. He returned to himself, not with certainty but with enough steadiness to move forward. We didn't speak because we didn't need to. The listening was not in words but in the breath, in the pause, in two nervous systems remembering what calm feels like in the safety of another.

After a while he stood, still nervous and still uncertain, but no longer alone in it. I stood beside him, quietly sure of one thing, that the breath we shared, that moment of quiet, was its own kind of listening, the kind that simply says I am here with you, even when there is nothing to say.

What happened between my son and me that morning, the slowing breath and the softening shoulders, was more than a tender pause in a hallway. It was a physiological shift, a wordless exchange beneath the quiet, a conversation in the body that spoke the language of safety.

This is co-regulation in action, not as theory but as something felt. Although it is often described in the context of infants and caregivers, it does not end with childhood. It grows with us and becomes something we can offer as much as receive. When someone is overwhelmed and the nervous system tips into urgency or collapse, what helps is rarely logic. What helps is the nearness of someone steady, someone whose presence asks for nothing, whose breath does not rush to fill the silence, and whose body quietly says I am here, you are not alone.

That morning I didn't try to talk my son out of his fear, and I didn't layer on reassurances or advice. I stayed with him, breathing and grounded, and his system responded, not because of what I said but because of how I was. This is how co-regulation works. It does not speak in sentences, it speaks in rhythm.

At the heart of it is the autonomic nervous system, especially the vagus nerve, the body's longest cranial nerve. It links the brainstem to the face, heart, lungs, and gut, and governs our instinctive defences such as fight, flight, or freeze, as well as our capacity to soften, settle, and connect. Dr Stephen Porges, whose Polyvagal Theory reshaped our understanding of connection, explains that our bodies are constantly scanning for cues of safety or danger. This process is not conscious but automatic, and he calls it neuroception, the body's intuitive radar. It does not weigh evidence or wait for proof, but listens for tone, for posture, for the flicker of a gaze, and for the cadence of a breath.

It listens to the other person's body and quietly asks whether it is safe, whether it can soften, whether it can come closer. When the answer is yes, even subtly, something shifts. The heart rate steadies, the jaw releases, and the shoulders lower almost imperceptibly. The nervous system begins to move out of defence, and the mind starts to return.

That is what happened in our hallway, not because I did something brilliant or therapeutic but because I didn't leave. I kept my breath slow enough for his to find its way back, two nervous systems in rhythm like tuning forks drawn into resonance.

This is not sentimentality, it is physiology. Research shows that moments of true attunement change the brain. When safety is restored, the amygdala, our internal alarm, grows quiet, and the prefrontal cortex, which supports reflection, impulse control, and perspective, comes back online. In these moments we do not simply feel better, we become more able to meet what is in front of us.[15]

And this, I have come to believe, is one of the most generous forms of listening we can offer. It is not a clever insight or the right words, but a presence that is real, grounded, and embodied. Such listening asks for patience, humility, and the willingness to be the calm in someone else's storm.

Because listening, in its deepest form, is not just an act but an offering, the felt sense that says you are not alone, I am here, you can let go. Sometimes this is the kind of listening that heals, not because it solves anything but because it reminds someone, quietly and steadily, that they do not have to carry this alone.

What struck me most about that moment with my son was how ordinary it was, how unremarkable it might have seemed from the outside, and yet how deeply familiar the feeling was. I had sensed it before, in other places and with other people. Co-regulation is not rare, nor is it reserved only for parent and child relationships or for therapeutic settings. It can happen anywhere, between anyone.

Different ways of listening

I have felt it beside a young woman on a flight, her breath sharp and uneven as panic rose when she realised she might miss her connection. I felt it again with a maintenance worker in the quiet of a back room, his shoulders hunched and eyes wet after the day had quietly broken him open. And I knew it once more crouched on the bathroom floor at a party, holding space for a friend unraveling behind a locked door.

In each of those moments, what helped was not advice or clever insight, nor strategy or any kind of brilliant intervention. What helped was presence and breath, not as instruction but as invitation. Let's breathe together. A simple phrase, a shared rhythm, a steadying anchor.

Just as I had done with my son, meeting panic with steadiness and fear with grounded breath, there was nothing flashy and nothing fixed. It was only breath, steady and soft, a nervous system saying what words could not, that you do not have to hold this alone. These were not grand moments but small acts of nervous system hospitality, quiet gestures and subtle offerings of safety. Yet in each one, something shifted, not because I resolved anything but because I stayed.

We tend to think of listening as something we do with our ears, an act of conscious attention, of decoding words and responding thoughtfully. Yet some of the deepest listening happens far below awareness, in the silent conversation between bodies. Long before we had language, we listened through rhythm and through the nervous system's quiet calibration, asking whether this person was safe to be near. Even now, our bodies are always tuning in, not only to what is said but to the energy beneath the words. At its core, listening is the art of sensing whether this is a space where we can soften.

This is where neuroscience meets what we might call presence. Neuroception does not wait for logic but detects and reacts. We do not need to analyse someone's expression to know that something is off, because we feel it in the body, a tightening in the chest, a subtle brace. At times we tense even in the company of someone familiar, and at other times we relax beside a stranger. The nervous system listens in ways the mind cannot fully name.

This kind of listening is not a special skill. It does not require training, only the willingness to stay near, to slow down, and to breathe. The body hears what language cannot say, and when we offer someone that kind of listening, grounded, steady, and without demand, we give them more than comfort, we give them back to themselves.

In the 1960s, psychologist Albert Mehrabian explored how meaning is conveyed when words, tone, and facial expression conflict. Today this is loosely referred to as the "7–38–55 rule." His research found that in emotionally ambiguous situations, meaning is conveyed roughly 7 percent through words, 38 percent through tone of voice, and 55 percent through facial expression and body language.[16] Crucially, these percentages apply

Different ways of listening

only when communicating feelings or attitudes, and only when verbal and nonverbal cues are incongruent, not to everyday discourse in general.

The percentages are not the point. The deeper insight is that when words and energy conflict, we trust the feeling beneath the sentence rather than the sentence itself. This is why "I'm fine" can land like a slammed door, why "Do whatever you want" can feel more like a dare than an invitation, and why silence, in just the wrong moment, can speak louder than anything said aloud.

We listen with our skin, with our gut, and with the hum of tension beneath the sternum that tightens when something does not quite add up. We notice the microexpressions and posture, the pause before a word is chosen, and the subtle falter of breath when something is left unsaid. Even when our conscious mind does not register it, the nervous system does.

In the tender places, such as moments of hurt, fear, or shame, the words might stay tidy but the body often does not. A clipped phrase, averted eyes, a breath held just a little too long, or a stillness that is not rest but bracing, all reveal the strain beneath the surface. These are not signs of deception but the nervous system doing what it was built to do, to protect.

Real listening begins here. Not with interpretation but with attunement, not with searching for the perfect response but with the willingness to notice the dissonance and remain with it. It is about sensing the shape of what is struggling to emerge and allowing space for it to arrive, even slowly. This is what Mehrabian's findings truly point to, that people do not need to be perfectly understood, they need to feel safe enough to speak from one place. When that safety is missing, the body knows, and it tenses, withholds, and fragments, not to confuse but to survive.

The real work of listening is not about decoding or diagnosing. It is about offering an undivided attention that allows someone to bring their full self into the room, one that does not demand they edit their truth in order to stay in relationship. When that kind of safety is felt, the nervous system begins to shift, what was guarded starts to soften, and what was scattered begins to cohere. In that softening, something rare becomes possible, and listening turns into more than a skill or an act of comprehension. It becomes communion.

There are times when words lose their grip, when emotion rises so fiercely it slips past language and what longs to be expressed has no shape, only sensation. Then it is the body that speaks, often through touch.

I was at a funeral once, in a modern chapel with sunlight spilling through stained glass. The air held a charged silence that felt less like absence and more like reverence. At the pulpit, the niece of the deceased began her tribute, her voice steady at first as she spoke of her uncle's kindness and of the time she had spent with him, her aunt, and her cousins.

Different ways of listening

Then, mid-sentence, her throat caught and her face crumpled as the words vanished. She tried, breath hitching, to find her way back, but the grief had overtaken her, and she stood there in silence, breaking open.

Before anyone else moved, her cousin, the son of the man being mourned, rose from the front row. Quietly and without hesitation, he walked toward her, calm and sure. He did not say a word but simply stood beside her and placed a hand on her shoulder, gentle and steady, fully human. That was all, no rescue, no redirection, no search for the right words, only connection.

Something shifted. Not everything, but enough, enough for her to breathe again, to steady herself, and to finish. It was one of the clearest expressions I have seen of listening without ears, of listening not to what was said but to what was held. He responded not to her collapse but to her vulnerability, and in doing so he offered something deeper than language, the quiet assurance that she did not have to hold this alone, that he was there.

Touch is one of our first languages. Before we can speak, we are held and rocked, soothed by warmth and rhythm, and our bodies remember. Even as adults we carry the knowing that touch, when safe and welcome, can calm what words cannot reach.

Science now affirms what we have always sensed. Supportive touch, whether a steady hand, a held palm, or a simple hug, helps the body settle. Oxytocin research shows that such contact fosters trust and bonding, while other studies confirm that stress hormones ease and the nervous system steadies. In one landmark study at the University of Virginia, people anticipating a stressful event showed significantly less threat response in the brain when they held a partner's hand.[17] Another paper published in *Adaptive Human Behavior and Physiology* reviewed evidence showing that even brief, gentle social touch can buffer physiological stress. Across multiple studies, affectionate touch was linked to lower heart rate and reduced cardiovascular reactivity in the face of acute stressors.[18]

This is not just comfort, it is co-regulation. Through touch we lend our nervous system to someone else, offering a steadier rhythm they can sync to when their own has gone ragged. Touch, however, is not only physical but relational, and the difference between feeling grounded and feeling jarred is not about how much pressure is applied, but about the nature of the exchange itself. What matters is not just what is given, but how it is offered.

That is why, in vulnerable moments, touch must be rooted in attunement and consent, since not everyone finds safety in contact. Yet when it is welcomed and offered with care, it becomes something sacred, a bridge between bodies and a wordless affirmation that says I see you, I feel what you are carrying, and I am here to help you hold it.

Sometimes, when words dissolve, a hand on the shoulder can say everything. In those moments listening becomes something different, something carried in breath, in stillness, in the quiet language of skin.

Different ways of listening

Black belt listening

I don't remember the exact day I got my black belt. I could probably look it up in an old journal, buried between stick-figure diagrams of techniques and training notes. But milestones like that do not really live on calendars, they live in the body.

What I remember most is the feeling, the bare feet pressing into the mat, the quiet give beneath each step. The air felt thicker than usual, not tense exactly but charged, as if it knew something I did not. I had been training for years, not only in movement but in attention, learning to listen with more than ears, with skin, with spine, with breath.

A few days earlier I had been told that grading would happen over the weekend. No exact time was given and there was no fanfare, because that was our tradition. You simply showed up, and when sensei sensed that something in you had settled, he would nod and say quietly, "You're ready," and then it would begin.

There was no announcement and no ceremony, only a shift in rhythm that was subtle but unmistakable. Sensei read from the list, one technique at a time, attackers stepping forward in turn. There was a script but no rehearsal, no time to pause, only motion. They grabbed and I moved, threw, reset, and repeated. Each call demanded precision, each partner brought a new timing and energy, and I had to meet it, blend, redirect, and stay centred. My breath deepened, my awareness sharpened, and the repetition pressed on my body and my mind, testing whether I could stay steady and adapt without freezing or forcing.

Within minutes I was sweating, not only from exertion but from the concentration it required. Every part of me felt alive, not tense but open. I was no longer thinking, because thought would have slowed me down and left me vulnerable. I was listening with my whole nervous system.

That is what Aikido teaches you if you stay long enough, and really what martial arts in general can teach if you let them. Listening is not passive and it is not polite nodding. It is a full-body discipline, a form of respect, a way of being fully present. In the middle of that grading I wasn't tracking words, I was tracking weight shifts, angles, breath. Every slight movement, a shift in balance, a tightening jaw, the lift of a heel was a sentence, and if I was tuned in I could hear it before it was spoken.

One of my seniors came in hard with a yokomen strike, a diagonal cut toward my head. There was no time to think, my body turned, my hands moved, and suddenly we were in motion, him airborne and me grounded. I hadn't planned it, I simply received it.

In that moment I saw that I hadn't spent all those years learning how to fight. I had been learning how to feel, how to meet energy without resisting it, overpowering it,

Different ways of listening

or trying to control it. How to stay with it, redirect it, remain connected, and let it speak.

That, to me, is black belt listening. It is not about mastery but about readiness, about knowing you no longer need to prove anything, about trusting the body more than the ego, and about letting failure shape you instead of frighten you.

By the time grading ended I was both exhausted and electric. Sensei and I sat facing each other on the mat, the other students quiet behind me. He spoke a few steady words, grounded and kind, naming what had gone well and offering reflections on what I could continue to work on, then asked me a couple of thoughtful questions. Finally, without ceremony, he picked up a folded piece of cloth and offered it to me.

The belt felt heavier than I expected, not because of the fabric but because of everything it carried, the mornings I did not want to train but did, the bruises and the doubts, the quiet and relentless hours of ukemi, learning to fall, to roll, to surrender to the mat.

It was not a symbol of achievement, it was an initiation. The belt seemed to say that now I was ready to begin, and that was the paradox. You work for years to earn the thing, and when you finally receive it you realise the real work is only just beginning.

Just like listening. You think you are good at it, nodding, making eye contact, reflecting back what someone says, and you think that is enough. Then someone sits across from you and speaks something raw, something that doesn't fit the script, and the practiced ways of responding no longer serve you or them. You realise this is different, that it is not a conversation but a moment, and you have to meet it with more than words.

Is anyone there?

Listening is not only something we do, it is something we show. Whether we intend to or not, we are always broadcasting through tone, posture, breath, and the way we make or avoid eye contact. Just as I have learned to read these signals in others, I have had to accept the truth that people are reading them in me as well.

One night my partner was telling me about her day. It was nothing dramatic, just a few irritations and a strange comment from a friend, the kind of ordinary download that carries its own intimacy. I nodded in the right places, murmured agreement, and added, "Ah, that's annoying" when it seemed appropriate. On the surface I looked engaged.

But I wasn't. Inside, my mind was spinning with thoughts about work, the message I had forgotten to reply to, and the task left unfinished. My body was still, yet my attention was somewhere else.

Different ways of listening

Then she stopped mid-sentence and said, "You're not listening, are you?" Her voice was not angry, only clear.

I froze. My reflex was to deflect and say, "Of course I am." I didn't, because I knew she was right, and more importantly, she knew it too. It was obvious not from anything I said but from everything else, my tone, the way my body leaned away, the vacant look on my face.

You cannot fake attention, not for long

That moment was humbling and clarifying. It reminded me that listening is not only about hearing but about how we show up, about what we transmit. The people we care about are listening with their whole nervous systems, and they know when we are only half there.

Since then I have realised there are really only two choices in moments like that. One is to catch myself, take a breath, let go of the mental noise, and re-enter the moment not only with my ears but with my whole body, leaning in so she can feel that I am here. The other is to name it kindly and honestly, saying, "I want to hear this, but my head is still stuck at work. Can we come back to it in fifteen minutes so I can be fully with you?"

Both are small acts of care, and both hold far more honesty than pretending ever could.

And there is science to back this up. We often think of listening as something passive, a quiet internal act of absorbing sound and meaning, yet research in communication, psychology, and neuroscience suggests otherwise. Listening is not only something we do, it is something others feel.

From the moment we enter a conversation we are communicating, whether we speak or not. The way we hold ourselves, the rhythm of our breath, the quality of our gaze, and even the tension in our face all send signals that are read consciously or unconsciously. Albert Mehrabian's research reminds us that when it comes to emotional content, words carry only a small part of the message, while tone and body language do most of the work. The same principle applies in reverse, because when we are the ones listening, we are also being read. Our tone, our stillness, and our posture all tell a story.

The nervous system is fast. Neuroscientific studies show that humans begin to register emotional facial expressions within a few hundred milliseconds, often well before conscious awareness. Long before the thinking brain has time to interpret, the emotional brain has already started to react. This innate and unconscious capacity allows us to sense safety or threat in someone's face, or in their voice as other research has shown, before a single word is fully processed.[19]

So when I sit with my partner and say all the right things like "I hear you" or "That makes sense," but my voice is tight, my posture guarded, and my eyes flick toward the clock, her nervous system registers something else, something truer, something louder. It does not matter that I meant well, because what matters is what I was communicating without even realising it.

Different ways of listening

People often say, "It's not what you said, it's how you said it," and they are right. How we show up is the message. Our body becomes the container for the conversation, and if that container is rushed, distracted, or carrying judgment, the other person's words or their vulnerability will never quite land. At worst, they may not even feel safe enough to try.

When our body softens and our breath slows, when our face shows that we are truly present, something shifts. The other person feels it. Their breathing changes, their voice steadies, and their nervous system, sensing safety, begins to open. This is not a technique. It is biology and relationship.

It also moves in the other direction. When someone does not feel heard, even when we believe we are listening, it may have little to do with our words and everything to do with our body quietly saying, "I am not really here."

Now, when I catch myself drifting, or when someone calls me out as my partner did that night, I try not to defend. Instead, I ask myself what my body is saying, what my tone and my breath are communicating, and whether I am truly making space for this person or only performing it.

The truth is that we are always listening, not just with our ears but with the whole of our attention. And others are listening to our listening as well.

Chapter 7.

Listening to your kids

I did not know I would love fatherhood this much. People had warned me about the sleepless nights, the tantrums, the endless requests for snacks, and the questions that somehow turn into philosophy at six in the morning. All of that arrived, along with the mess, the noise, and the slow erosion of solitude. Yet something else arrived too, something I did not expect. Threaded through a three a.m. diaper change or rising suddenly out of the chaos of airborne spaghetti was joy, not just fleeting amusement but full-bodied, messy, laugh-while-cleaning-the-wall joy.

I have two boys, and from the beginning they have wrecked and rebuilt my world in ways I never knew I needed. Every night we wrestled on the floor until someone, usually me, was stepped on and we called a time-out. We rode bikes through the neighbourhood like a small superhero gang, built Lego towers only to destroy them with delight, and turned bath time into a strategy game. Bedtime stories always stretched longer than planned, yet I never really minded. There was a rhythm to it all, a kind of rough and loving poetry, and woven into that rhythm was a constant stream of interruption.

"Daddy. Daddy. Daddy!"

It did not matter if I was mid-thought, elbow-deep in peanut butter, or finishing a sentence on the phone, they would come rushing in, full-hearted and immediate, completely absorbed in whatever had just entered their universe. At first I told myself I was handling it well, that I was being patient, yet the truth is I was often only waiting for the interruption to pass, itching to return to the thread I believed mattered more.

One day I saw it differently. I had just asked one of them, gently I thought, to wait, telling him, "Hang on buddy, I'm talking to someone." In that moment I noticed his shoulders dip, not dramatically enough to draw attention but just enough to show that something in him had dimmed. He was not angry. He had simply faded, and I felt the quiet ache of it land. He did not need me to stop everything, only to know he still existed within my field of attention.

So I tried something new. I would look up, meet their eyes, and say, "Let me finish this, and in 5 minutes I'm all yours," and then I made sure to follow through, every time. The shift was not in the words themselves but in the consistency, the quiet promise that I would return and that their presence had not been erased by mine. Gradually the interruptions softened, not out of fear of consequence but out of trust in the connection. They knew they would be seen.

Listening to your kids

There is science behind this. Research shows that when children feel not only noticed but truly met, their nervous systems begin to settle, and they learn safety through presence and consistency rather than through perfection or performance.[19] Psychologist Dan Siegel calls this "mindsight," the ability to feel felt, which serves as a cornerstone of emotional resilience. It does not require a profound parenting breakthrough, only a pause and a turning toward.

Sometimes I think about Aikido and how the body listens before the mind has a chance to catch up. On the mat you do not respond to words but to pressure, timing, and the subtle arc of someone's intent, learning to connect without bracing and to blend without losing yourself. This is still how I try to meet my sons, even though they are no longer so little.

They are seventeen and fifteen now, no longer children but young men, testing edges and carrying their own gravity. These days there is more talking than wrestling, with dinner conversations, YouTube solo camping videos, and sarcasm tossed across the table like a lazy frisbee. At times we still ride bikes or head to the football, shoulders brushing in the crowd, and I feel, maybe even more strongly now, how much it matters that I listen.

It is not always their words I am listening to but their signals and silences, the sideways glances that seem to ask, "I'm not sure if it's safe to say this out loud." Some days I miss these cues and stay buried in the task, pushing through whatever feels urgent. More often, though, I notice the tug and the pause, the small invitation to turn toward them.

When I allow my attention to land fully, I find I do not always need words. My gaze carries what my mouth might fumble and says, I see you, I am here, you matter more than this screen. Something in them opens, not in the way it did when they were five and curled into my lap, but in a quieter current, a kind of silent exhale.

I keep learning that listening to your kids does not end when they stop asking questions. It simply shifts to a different frequency, the volume lower but the need still present. They want to be seen not for who we imagine they might become but for who they already are, in all their contradictions and in all their becoming.

Maybe the real work now is to keep listening, especially in the moments when they go quiet.

Seeing eye to eye

He was maybe four, flushed and clenched-fisted, with tears brimming just beneath the heat in his face.

"I hate you."

Three words, sharp and heavy, thrown like a stone. It was over something small, bedtime perhaps, one of those ordinary moments that suddenly fracture. I stood in the hallway with my pulse quickening and my breath caught between disbelief and the urge to restore order. For a moment I wanted to clamp down, not to punish since that has never been my instinct, but to control with a sharper tone, a firmer posture, something that would mark the line.

Then I saw his face, his small frame rigid with emotion too big for his body and his jaw locked not in defiance but in an effort to keep from breaking. In that instant something loosened inside me where my reaction might have taken hold. He was not trying to hurt me. He was hurting, and he did not yet have the words for it. He could not say, "I feel overwhelmed," or "I don't know how to handle this boundary," or "I need you to help me hold what's flooding through me," so he reached for the only thing that gave him even a flicker of power.

"I hate you."

It took everything in me to stay with him, to resist meeting force with force, to hold back the urge to correct or explain or shrink the moment into something tidy. Instead I crouched, met him at eye level, and let my voice settle into the ground.

"You seem really upset."

He did not speak or collapse into me, yet he did not turn away either. We stayed like that, eye to eye and breath to breath, until the heat began to soften and the silence stretched between us. Then, without a word, he leaned in and folded against me, spent.

That moment rewired something in me. What had once looked like disrespect I began to see as distress. Children do not arrive with emotional blueprints. They feel first, raw and fast and unsorted, and when it overflows it often spills out sideways in the form of shouting, shutting down, or lashing out. They are not testing us. They are reaching, and behind the slammed doors and wild words rests a question that matters deeply. Can you stay with me, even now?

My own question became whether I could be the one who stays. Not the fixer or the enforcer, but the one who listens without needing the storm to pass on schedule. That does not mean anything goes, since boundaries still matter, yet presence changes their texture. Boundaries rooted in fear feel brittle, while boundaries held with connection land differently, more like scaffolding than threat.

When I remembered to lead with, "I'm here. I see you. We'll get through this," something in them softened. It did not happen instantly, but it happened reliably. I stopped asking myself how to make it stop and began to wonder what was underneath it. At times it was fear, at other times hunger, and often it was the impossible bigness of being small in a fast-moving world. The more I tuned in to the signal beneath the noise, the less they needed to shout.

That is still the work, not to manage but to meet, not to anticipate every rupture but to remain reachable inside it, not to perfect the moment but to hold it. Beneath every outburst rests a quiet question, asking if you can handle all of me, even this part.

And when the answer is yes, even if it is offered imperfectly and quietly, they begin to learn something that lasts. I do not have to be easy to be loved.

Don't be so dramatic

You see it everywhere, at parks, in cafés, during school pick-ups, small moments that are easy to miss unless you are watching closely. A child says something awkward, emotional, or unfinished, and the parent quickly steps in with a correction, a reframe, or a small lesson such as saying it is not that bad, asking them not to speak that way, reminding them to say thank you properly, or taking over the task with a quick let me just do it. None of this is unkind. It comes from care, from love, from the desire to help children grow into thoughtful and emotionally intelligent humans, and I understand that pull because I have felt it myself. Yet there is also a tension in it, a hurriedness, as if the moment is too raw to be left alone.

I once watched a girl of about seven standing beside her mother in line at a bookstore, cradling a book with visible excitement as she bounced on her toes. Loud enough for a few people to hear she said, "I think this book is going to change my life." For a moment there was only silence, the wild and beautiful weight of her sincerity hanging in the air. Her mother smiled and replied gently, "Sweetheart, don't be so dramatic." The girl blinked and seemed to shrink slightly, her eyes dropping to the book as her voice fell quiet. It was not a harsh reply, yet something in her softened in the wrong way, as though a window had been pulled closed.

I do not know their story, and this is not about blame, but I noticed what happened in the silence that followed rather than in the words themselves. The air seemed to tighten, and something in the girl quietly closed.

I have come to believe that every child carries a developing inner voice, and in the early years that voice is often borrowed from us, shaped by what we say and how we say it and by what we allow to live in the spaces between. When we fill every gap, correct every misstep, and smooth over every wobble, that voice has little room to grow, remaining reactive and hesitant, dependent on external regulation. Yet when we allow, not by approving but simply by making space, that voice begins to find its own rhythm.

It is not easy, and I have lost count of the times I stepped in with a suggestion or tried to help my sons rephrase something, especially in public when their behaviour felt as though it might reflect on me. There is a deep vulnerability in allowing our children to remain in process, particularly when that process is messy, awkward, or unfinished. Yet something different begins to unfold when we resist the urge to fix.

I remember one of my boys, maybe ten at the time, trying to build something with his hands, and it was not going well. The pieces were too small and his fingers not quite steady, frustration showing in his breath and in the tension across his shoulders. I sat nearby with every part of me wanting to step in, to offer a tip, to nudge him past the stuck point, yet I stayed still. He did not ask for help and I did not offer. I simply remained close until, after a few more scrambles and sighs, he paused, sat back, looked at the mess, and said that he thought he needed a break.

That was it, no outburst and no meltdown, only a flicker of self-awareness, a moment of self-regulation, a seed of emotional maturity that would never have had the chance to bloom if I had stepped in too soon. This is what becomes possible when we let go of the urge to fix. It is not passivity or indifference, but trust in their ability to learn from the world and in our ability to stay near without steering everything.

Sometimes the best way to help is not to help at all. What they need is often less about our guidance and more about our gaze, steady, calm, and undemanding. The greatest gift can be space, the space to become while we remain near, not fixing or guiding but simply staying. And in offering that to them, we also relearn how to offer it to ourselves.

A test

It was just a test, but not to him. He walked into the kitchen slower than usual, carrying the quiet heaviness children hold when something has not gone the way they hoped. His shoulders dipped as he set down his bag with care, as if even that small movement required gentleness. I looked up and asked how it had gone. He did not meet my eyes as he said, "Forty-eight percent," and then, almost apologetically, added, "I really tried." I believed him, because I had seen the notes and the long afternoons spent hunched over a textbook that never seemed to open the right door. This was not about effort but about fit, a subject that refused to speak his language no matter how much he wanted it to.

I felt the reflex stir, the urge to soften the blow with perspective, to say something comforting like it is just one test or you will bounce back. But I caught myself and instead asked, "How do you feel?" He did not answer right away, only stood there holding the weight of the moment in his chest, and I waited, not to fix or steer but to remain with him long enough for something true to emerge. Eventually he said, "I'm really disappointed. I just don't get it." I had no fix for that. I could not make economics make sense even to myself, let alone to him, and I could not lift the weight of his disappointment, but perhaps that was not what he needed.

Listening to your kids

What he needed was room, not reassurance or interpretation, but space for his own clarity to surface. So I stayed, and gradually something in him shifted, a deeper breath, a small change in posture, a quieting of whatever had been bracing inside him. Then he said, "I think I'd like a tutor." I nodded and replied, "Okay. Let's organise that."

It was such a small moment, with no big insight and no emotional crescendo, yet it stayed with me. What mattered was not the words themselves but what was allowed to unfold. I realised that this is the real work, not always saying the right thing but holding the silence that allows someone else to find what is real.

Psychologist Lisa Feldman Barrett teaches that emotions are not simply felt but constructed, shaped both by experience and by how others meet us in moments of feeling. Our emotional vocabulary grows less from explanation and more from repeated exposure to safety, and children do not learn to process disappointment because we talk them through it. They learn because someone stays, showing them again and again that their inner world does not need to be rushed, fixed, or hidden.

That is what I have come to believe, especially as my boys have grown. When we meet their struggle with presence instead of pressure, and when we bring curiosity instead of control, we are not only helping them through a hard moment but also building the scaffolding for how they will meet themselves.

Katherine Reynolds Lewis puts it simply, when we shift from compliance to connection we raise children who regulate themselves not out of fear but through practice. They learn that emotional ground does not collapse beneath them and they learn they can stay. That day my son did not need comfort, he needed clarity of his own. Because I did not rush to explain or wrap the moment in meaning, he found it quietly and on his own terms. This is what presence offers, not a fix but a field, an openness that allows something true to arrive.

And as much as my children benefit from this, I have come to see how much I do as well. The more I practice staying with them without rushing or rescuing, the more I notice how often I try to do the same to myself, smoothing discomfort, wrapping it in language, and making it neat before it has even fully formed.

Sometimes, when I catch myself, I pause and ask the same question I once asked him, "How do you feel?" Then I wait, not for insight or closure but simply long enough for the truth to settle, because even now, with all I have learned, I am still learning how to feel things all the way through. And my children, in their honest and unguarded way, are still teaching me how.

Chapter 8.

Listening to your partner

It had been a year since Junko and I separated, but I was still in the house, sleeping in the spare room with the door mostly closed, moving through our old routines with a kind of quiet reverence. My youngest would still ask, "Can I sleep in Daddy's room?" then curl up beside me as if it were a sleepover. He moved in his sleep, warm and restless, and for those few hours, the house felt less divided. We did not speak about the change directly, but I think he felt it too.

Junko and I were still raising the boys together, doing our best to stay respectful and kind, but something essential had gone quiet between us. We both felt it, even if we rarely said so.

There is something surreal about waking each morning inside the echo of a life that no longer fully includes you. I told myself I was staying for the boys, hoping to soften the transition and keep the sharp edges from cutting too deep. Maybe that was partly true. But underneath that reason, I already knew it would be me who would have to leave. I would be the one to pack my things, step out of the house, and begin again.

The harder truth was that I was afraid. Afraid to let go completely, to face the blank page, to be alone with whatever came next. And the truth is, you cannot begin a new chapter while still sleeping across the hall from the one that just ended.

One quiet afternoon, I signed a lease on a small apartment just across the street. It had a narrow kitchen, secondhand furniture, and the mattress from the spare room I had been sleeping in. Nothing about it was fancy, but it was mine. The boys loved it. They stayed three, sometimes four nights a week, and quickly turned the space into something that felt like a sleepover party. We cooked pasta, rode bikes, played two-square, and fell asleep in crumb-sticky piles of limbs and laughter. It was chaotic and tender, and it felt real.

And then they would leave, heading back to their mum, and the silence would return. Not the peaceful kind, but the kind that buzzes from the fridge light at midnight and lingers in the corners of space that still feels half empty.

Eventually, I gave online dating a try. There were swipes, short bios, and half-hearted conversations that disappeared almost as soon as they began. The whole thing felt like applying for love through a job portal. Then a friend, always the instigator, suggested I try speed dating.

"You'll love it," he said. "It's weird, awkward, human. At least it's not an app."

So I went.

I arrived early, as I usually did, and ordered a drink. There is something about holding a glass that makes waiting feel a little less exposed. I turned to look around, and there she was.

She walked in like late summer, bright and effortless, with a softness that carried its own gravity. Her dress was light and sheer, clinging just enough to trace the shape of her body. She was stunning, elegant without effort, the kind of beauty that does not need to perform because it simply exists. When she sat nearby, the air seemed to shift around her, it was not lust or fantasy, it was a sense of stillness, the kind that quiets something inside you.

I asked if I could join her, and her smile came quickly. It was warm and unguarded, more an invitation than a reply. "Sure," she said, and I sat down, already aware that something had quietly begun.

Her name was Antoinette. From the moment we began talking, it felt as if we were stepping into a conversation that had already been waiting for us. We spoke about meditation, psychology, and personality types, wandering easily from one thought to the next. She was sharp and soulful, carried a warm sense of humour, and with her Italian roots and unforced beauty she had a way of disarming without even trying.

Then the host called out, "Ladies to booths, men will rotate." She slipped into one before I could catch up, which meant I wouldn't see her again until the very last round of the night.

Speed dating surprised me. When you listen without scanning for compatibility or preparing your own story, five minutes can hold more than you might expect. People tend to open up when they feel met with genuine curiosity instead of performance.

I kept count of the rounds, waiting for the moment I could return to her. When it finally came, the rhythm between us picked up right where it had left off, only now there was a shift, a subtle tilt, a smile that lingered a little longer. We sat a little closer, the space between us quietly changed.

The bell rang to signal the end of our five minutes, but we barely noticed. Time had softened at the edges. Twenty minutes passed before the host announced the event was over and pointed upstairs for anyone who wanted to keep talking. We didn't respond. We just stood and moved together, as if the decision had already been made.

It was a weeknight, and the evening had stretched later than we expected. I offered to walk her to her car. When we reached the curb, we exchanged numbers. There was a quiet pause, then a kiss, soft and unhurried. It came with no promise, only a sense of quiet attention. But something in it made clear that this mattered.

We have been together ever since.

Listening to your partner

That night marked something more than just meeting her, even though she was the spark. What changed was the choice I made afterward. I told myself this time I would listen. Not the kind of listening that waits for a turn to speak, or the kind that jumps in to fix or analyse. Just a quieter kind of listening that stays.

I listened not only to her words, but also to her energy, her pauses, her fury, and her silence. After the quiet, often unspoken rhythm of a Japanese marriage, loving Antoinette, expressive and passionate and alive in every gesture, felt like trading the stillness of a koi pond for the raw force of a storm.

But I was ready for the weather.

I do not always get it right, still reaching to explain too soon or trying to soothe what needs room to breathe. More often now I notice, sometimes in the moment and sometimes only afterward. It feels like Aikido, where you miss, then recover, and keep moving with what is there. With time, it stops being a technique and begins to feel like a return.

Listening for the need

It was early in our relationship, maybe two or three months in, and we were lying on the couch one night with a movie playing that neither of us was really watching. Her legs rested across my lap while a soft after-dinner stillness settled around us. A small flicker of misunderstanding had just passed between us, the kind that could have tipped into an argument if we had leaned in too hard, but instead we paused and allowed the heat to dissolve.

In the quiet that followed, I said, "There's something I've been practicing called Nonviolent Communication or NVC for short. It has helped me slow down and listen in a different way, and I wonder if it might be useful for us."

She turned toward me, neither defensive nor eager, simply present. "Tell me about it," she said.

I did not offer a framework or diagrams, only the heart of it. Behind most conflict lies an unmet need, and often we react from pain before we even realise we are hurting. If we can learn to speak from that place, the longing and the ache, the part that still wants connection even in fear, then something begins to change.

She nodded slowly. "That makes sense." A small smile spread across her face, soft and a little tilted. "But it sounds hard."

"It is," I said, smiling back. It is one thing to understand NVC and another to live it, especially with the person who holds your heart. We tried, not perfectly and not always, but with intention.

When I opened up, which happened more often than I expected, it was usually about the boys. A moment that struck deeper than I admitted, something one of them said or left unsaid, feelings I could not yet name, with pride and guilt, joy and worry woven into a single thread. Speaking it aloud helped me trace its shape. At times Antoinette met me there, not with advice or tidy resolutions but with a listening that gave the feelings space. Her questions came slowly and without agenda, asking what I thought it might have meant for him, how it had felt for me, or whether I wanted to sit with it in silence or talk it through.

Not every time, but often enough that I could feel her trying, and that mattered. At other times she slipped into solution mode, and I did too, the old reflex to fix or clarify still surfacing when emotions ran high or time felt short. Even when the words missed, the effort did not. Her care was there, along with her attention and her willingness to stay with me, and in the end that was enough.

I tried to offer her the same. When she came home from work tight with stress, I often rushed in with three solutions before she had even taken off her shoes. I thought I was helping, clearing the fog and lifting the weight, but I could see in her body that it landed differently. Her shoulders would pull back, her eyes dim slightly, and I knew that was not what she needed. So I would pause, exhale, and reset. "Sorry, that was an unsolicited opinion. Please continue." Sometimes she smiled, other times it was just a breath, a small nod, and a quiet, "Thanks. I wasn't looking for advice. I just needed to say it out loud." In those moments something between us would ease, not resolved but less tense, less lonely.

Listening in a relationship is not about never missing, it is about noticing when you do and choosing to return, not with defense or polish but with presence. Research supports this. Decades of studies on couples show that what sustains love is not the absence of conflict but the willingness to repair.[20] The Gottman Institute puts it simply. Repair is the strongest predictor of lasting connection, and it does not begin with solutions, it begins with listening.

That is what NVC has shown me, not as a script to follow or a philosophy to recite, but as a posture, an embodied practice of staying connected to what is alive in me, in her, and in the delicate space between us. It invites questions before conclusions, asking what I am really feeling, what lies underneath that, and what the other person might be needing as well.

Sometimes we come close and other times we miss completely, yet we keep trying, and more importantly, we return. This relationship, like the practice itself, is not about perfection. It is about remaining reachable, staying real, and choosing to stay with it.

We do not speak NVC like natives, but we know it well enough to find our way back. We pause before reacting, we say, "Let's try again," and we mean it. That is what love feels like now, not clean or simple, but full of grace and full of effort. Two people, flawed and awake, still evolving, learning to hear each other more deeply, even when it is hard. In-fact, especially when it is hard.

The cost of being right

It usually begins with something small. A detail I insist on clarifying. "I didn't say Tuesday, I said Wednesday." Or, "That's not exactly how it happened."

Not loud or cruel, just precise. The same precision I'd learned to listen past when a partner said "I'm fine." I was now weaponizing it in reverse.

The words sound measured, but I can see the effect. She pulls back slightly, her voice thins, and the ease between us begins to fade. The conversation dims, no longer about the story we were sharing but about how I've begun to shape it.

Eventually I notice, usually a beat too late, and the low murmur of regret begins to stir. I ask myself, quietly and inwardly, why I said it and what I thought it would accomplish.

I was not trying to hurt her or to win. What I wanted was to stay in control, to hold on to the facts, the framing, and the way the moment was remembered. Over time I learned that control is the opposite of connection. That lesson did not arrive all at once but through friction and the slow repetition of tiny ruptures, each one too small to name yet undeniable in the pattern they created.

I started to trace the thread back, not just in our conversations but in myself. That quiet, compulsive drive to tighten the facts, to clarify, adjust, and explain, especially when I felt exposed, had been with me for years. I don't think I inherited it, but I do remember how it began. A regional enrolment mix-up meant I started school a year younger than everyone else, and I spent years trying to prove I belonged. I wanted to sound older, smarter, more certain than I was. The impulse became armour. If I could control the story, I believed I would be safe from misunderstanding, from blame, and from the shame of being seen as less than enough.

Our nervous systems do not respond to logic. They respond to tone, rhythm, and the quiet signals that let us know whether we are being received or revised. Even a gentle correction can feel like dismissal, a small fracture in trust, a subtle message that says we are not being felt but managed.

Listening to your partner

Presence matters more than precision, and Gottman's research echoes the same truth. It is not conflict that erodes relationships but defensiveness, the subtle edge in the voice or the reflex to counter instead of stay with. Over time the space between two people narrows, not with intimacy but with caution.

I've been on the receiving end too. You open up, uncertain and still forming thoughts, only to have someone tidy your experience into their version. The same thing that happened when I once said "I'm fine" and someone replied, "No you're not, you're just tired." Dismissing what I actually felt.

Each time, something closes. Not dramatically, but with an internal click. You might nod, even smile, and shift the conversation, but something pulls back. Not punishment but self-protection. You don't feel heard. You feel edited.

Now I try to meet those moments differently. Recently, Antoinette and I were recalling something that happened at a friend's dinner, a small miscommunication involving the boys. She described it in a way that did not match my memory, and I felt the reflex surge, hot and immediate. The words almost left my mouth, ready to correct her. Instead, I paused and looked at her, not just listening to the story but to the feeling underneath. I could see it in her face, the emotion, the weight, and the unspoken echo of what the moment had meant.

I chose not to correct her but to stay with her, letting the moment stay alive. We kept talking, and in that continuation the air between us changed. Quiet but unmistakable. She never spoke of it again, yet I could feel the ease return in her voice and see it in the way her body leaned toward me rather than away.

When we feel heard, the grip releases. Trust drifts back quietly, without announcement. What stays with me is how easily the moment could have gone differently. The hidden cost of needing to be right shows itself in subtle interruptions that land as slights, exchanges that close instead of open, stories left unfinished because we are too busy trying to hold the pen.

The gift of restraint is where connection lives, held not in the accuracy of details but in the accuracy of presence. Yet there are still moments when I want to pause and ask, "What did you hear me say?" I would not ask to challenge or trap, but because I know how easily words can become distorted, shaped not by malice but by memory, fear, and the old wounds that bend meaning before it even lands.

Sometimes I speak with care, slow and intentional, only to hear a response that feels like it belongs to another conversation altogether. A part of me wants to protest, to insist, "That is not what I meant." Yet in a way it is, because none of us hear in isolation. Every word passes through history before it reaches us.

It hurts to be interpreted rather than received. When someone insists, "I know what you really meant," with absolute certainty, I find myself thinking, *Do you? Did you ask?* That is not listening, it is projection. These days I sometimes try another way. I ask gently, "Can you tell me what you heard?" And when the words that return carry even part of the intention I meant to share, something eases. My body softens, the air feels lighter, and the moment releases its tension.

If the reply comes back far from what I meant, I do not correct or argue. I simply say, "That is not what I was trying to say. Let me try again." Then I keep going, offering it in different words until what I hear reflected back carries the shape of what I intended. No shortcuts, no need to win, just the slow work of staying with it until understanding feels honest rather than assumed.

When that happens, when what I say is finally carried back in a way that feels true, I am reminded that real understanding is not about perfect agreement. It is about alignment. And that, more than being right, is what most of us are longing for.

Listening as a love language

I once believed love was something you proved through action, whether by holding the door, cooking the meal, or saying the right thing at the right time. Over the years I have learned those things still matter, yet they are not the whole story. I bring Antoinette her coffee in the morning and rub her shoulders when she is stiff from work. We hold hands as we walk, even when silence stretches between us. I believe in gestures, small and steady, that carry the message I see you, even if I sometimes need reminding.

But the longer I have been in this relationship, and the more I have practiced listening within it, the more I have come to understand something deeper. Listening may be one of the most essential ways we say I love you. Not with the well-timed nod, the tilted head, or the gentle "I hear you," which can so easily become performance, a way of managing conversation rather than entering it. I mean a slower kind of listening, the kind that softens the room and stays steady even when the words come out tangled or the emotions run hot. It is the kind that says I care more about understanding you than proving myself. I want to feel what you are feeling, not only hear what you are saying. I will stay, even if it gets messy.

When Antoinette and I find that kind of listening, not perfectly but with honesty, the atmosphere between us shifts. The air feels weighted in a way that brings ease, the moment stretches, and there is space to breathe even in disagreement. Sometimes it arrives quietly. I will share something with her, a moment that stirred more in me than I expected, and she will not interrupt or rush to solve it. She simply lets the moment unfold, and I can feel her presence resting between us like a hand held gently in place. In that contact, something inside me settles.

At other times the moment carries more charge. One of us is tense, reactive, caught in the familiar loop of circling the same argument. Yet even then, if one of us pauses long enough to say, "I think we're spiraling," and the other is willing to hear it, the tone begins to change. By naming what lives beneath the surface, we loosen the grip of the loop and make room for something new to emerge.

This is what love has come to mean for me. It is not only warmth or affection but the willingness to stay, especially when things are hard. Deepak Chopra describes presence as "attention without judgment," a kind of space that lets another person's experience be exactly what it is, without the pressure to correct or improve it. Marshall Rosenberg added that when we give someone our full attention without fixing or filtering, we meet one of the most basic human needs, which is the need to be heard.

Research affirms this. A study in the *Journal of Experimental Social Psychology* found that people who felt deeply listened to experienced greater clarity, stronger validation, and an increased sense of self-worth, not because their problems had been solved but because their experience had been honored.[21] Another study from the University of Haifa showed that high-quality listening encouraged people to share difficult emotions, not because the subject itself felt safe but because the space in which they were held did.[22]

When people feel genuinely listened to, they begin to speak with honesty rather than polish. What comes forward is not the rehearsed version but the unguarded truth, and that is where closeness begins to take root. Gottman's research shows that emotional responsiveness, the steady act of turning toward a partner's cues, is one of the strongest predictors of lasting love. It is not agreement or resolution that sustains a bond, but the simple willingness to keep turning toward one another.

Looking back at earlier relationships, I can see how often I failed to grasp this. I believed I was helping when I offered insight, perspective, or what I thought was a clearer path forward. What I was really doing was managing my own discomfort, arranging emotions into something I could handle, and listening only enough to steer the moment toward stability. I was not trying to control the person I was with, yet I was trying to control the space, and while it was not malicious, it was not love.

Love does not sound like, "Here's what you should do." It sounds more like, "I'm with you, tell me more." Often it does not sound like words at all. It is the kind of silence that does not pull away, a silence that stays and holds steady, offering its presence without needing to fix or fill the space.

Over time I have come to see that listening is one of the most faithful ways love shows itself. It is the way love reaches across distance and says, I am still here, even when nothing can be solved. It may not be glamorous and it does not always feel profound, yet it is steady and real, and far more often than we admit, it is what makes the difference.

If you want to know whether someone feels loved, do not ask if they are happy. Ask if they feel heard. A relationship can run smoothly for years, with bills paid, tasks divided, and schedules aligned, and yet leave one or both people feeling deeply alone. Love is not sustained by logistics. It lives in recognition, in the felt experience

Listening to your partner

of being known, not for what you provide but for who you are.

Antoinette and I still miss each other at times, but we keep trying. On the days when I say the wrong thing, give advice instead of space, or am unsure how else to show love, I return to a simple practice. I listen. Not to fix or guide or prove anything, but to stay near, to make space, and to show up.

Because listening is how we find our way back to each other. It happens in silence, in difficulty, in the simple decision to stay when it would be easier to turn away. Perhaps that is what love really is. Not the absence of rupture, but the steady willingness to return, again and again.

Chapter 9.

Listening at work

I had just turned forty-four when we sold the company. It should have felt like freedom, a moment to begin again, open and unstructured. But I wasn't drawn to starting something new. What I wanted was to join something already in motion, to be part of something I didn't have to build alone.

After years of making the decisions, I was ready to find out who I might be without holding the reins. I took a leadership role at a web development agency as Chief Experience Officer. It was a title they had never used before, and one I had never held. I wasn't entirely sure what it meant, but I was curious. I wanted to know if I could contribute without being the one to shoulder all the weight.

Two months in, we held a leadership offsite retreat. The setting felt relaxed, but the purpose ran deeper than it appeared. It was the kind of gathering designed to align the culture and assess the team as a whole. One exercise in particular stayed with me. Each person was plotted on a quadrant grid measuring two dimensions: cultural fit and performance. Those who scored high on both were considered A-players. Those who fell low on both were seen as unlikely to remain.

When it was time for the leadership team to evaluate me, I stepped out of the room. That was the usual process. They discussed while I waited in the hallway, watching a spider rebuild its web above the doorframe. When I came back in, I glanced at the whiteboard and saw my initials in the top left quadrant, high marks for culture, low for performance. A steady B-player.

I blinked, drew a slow breath, and let it settle like weather. It was honest, but not personal. I didn't flinch or try to explain the invisible work it had taken to find my rhythm in a new system. I just listened as they said the role was still too new to measure, and that they were still learning how to understand its value.

I nodded and said, "Once the role becomes more defined, and you've had more time to see me in it, the basis for that rating will probably shift." That was all. No pitch. No list of bullet points to prove my value.

Shoulders relaxed around the table. A few people nodded in quiet agreement. The atmosphere changed. One person offered a small, almost apologetic smile. The shift was subtle, not toward certainty but toward something steadier. It felt like respect.

Looking back, that moment taught me more about listening at work than any strategy session ever had. The listening was not just directed outward, but inward as well. I could feel the old reflex flickering in my chest, the urge to prove something, to win approval, to perform. I knew that version of myself well, the one who believed belonging had to be earned by being the best in the room. But this time, I let that version step back. I chose to stay present instead.

I let the feedback land and gave the uncertainty room to breathe. I didn't shrink or push but stayed with it, and something shifted, not only in how they saw me but in how I began to hold myself.

We often carry a myth into professional spaces, the belief that being a good communicator means being articulate, persuasive, and quick on your feet. That listening is just a strategic pause before offering a stronger idea. But real listening, the kind that builds trust and slowly reshapes culture from within, moves differently. It does not seek attention. It is not a performance.

It begins as a choice in the nervous system, a decision that takes place beneath language. It means not flinching when you are misunderstood, not spiralling when someone misreads you, and not rushing to correct the version of yourself they have imagined. It is the decision to stay, not out of passivity, but out of presence.

From that quiet steadiness, something starts to shift. It does not always show, and it rarely happens all at once, but people feel it. Slowly, and often without knowing why, they begin to listen in return.

Seek first to understand

It took me years to understand that listening is not just one aspect of leadership. It is leadership. Not the kind you see on keynote stages or read about in polished mission statements. Not the kind that dazzles with clarity or rallies with charisma. I mean something quieter, less visible, and more essential. It is the kind of leadership you can sense in a room before anyone speaks. The kind that creates safety, not through slogans or systems, but through presence. Slow, unseen and real.

When I first read *The 7 Habits of Highly Effective People*, I paused at the fifth habit and read it again. Seek first to understand, then to be understood. It didn't feel like ordinary advice. It felt like an invitation, a quiet dare that challenged the kind of leadership I had come to accept, not because anyone had taught it to me directly but because I had absorbed it from the world around me.

I used to believe that leadership was about having the answers, having a plan, being the one others turned to in moments of uncertainty. Listening felt like a helpful soft skill, a way to collect input before making the real decisions. But over time, through trial, error, and the often uncomfortable process of learning, I began to see it differently. Listening is not soft. It is structural. It is the ground that holds everything else in place. Without it, nothing truly connects. Alignment, innovation, accountability, and strategy all depend on people feeling heard, not just acknowledged but understood in a way that allows them to lower their guard and bring more of themselves to the work.

The further you move into leadership, the less honesty tends to surround you. People begin to filter their words, holding back feedback, questioning their instincts, and often saying what they think you want to hear. This is rarely done with ill intent, it happens because power changes the atmosphere, and over time, many people learn that it feels safer to stay quiet around it. If you are not paying close attention, you can miss the shift. You assume things are going well, hear agreement where there is actually withdrawal, and mistake politeness for clarity. Eventually, you realise the room is still full, but no one is truly with you.

That is what Covey was pointing toward. Seek first to understand is not a technique, it is a posture. It asks you to enter the conversation with humility, to accept that you do not already know everything that matters, and to recognise that something essential may still be hidden from view. It means slowing the part of you that wants to be respected, long enough to earn someone's trust. It means listening in a way that brings steadiness. Not just to hear someone, but to create the kind of space where they feel safe enough to keep speaking.

This is not easy, especially in roles where we have been trained to solve problems, offer guidance, and lead from the front. Silence can feel uncomfortable. Uncertainty can seem like a weakness. So we rush to fill the space and move toward clarity before the truth has even had a chance to emerge. But if you can stay with the discomfort, if you can hold the tension of not knowing, something deeper begins to reveal itself. You start to notice the pause before a sentence, the tightness in someone's shoulders, the thing they almost say but hold back.

When you resist the urge to rescue or redirect, and instead stay rooted in the moment, something begins to open. I have seen it in rooms that felt stuck for weeks, circling the same safe talking points, until someone, often without warning, finally names what no one else wanted to say. It is not that they suddenly found more courage. It is that the atmosphere shifted, and the person leading the room did not interrupt, did not explain. They simply stayed quiet and present, long enough for the truth to feel safe.

I have also been the leader who missed those moments. I have nodded with interest while my mind was elsewhere, asked for feedback while quietly holding on to my own conclusions, and listened just enough to reply but not enough to truly understand. I can feel the difference now, not just in my own body, but in the space between people. When a leader listens with real curiosity, without an agenda or the need to perform, the room begins to shift. The atmosphere settles, people lean in and offer something real, not because they are told to, but because they trust it will be received.

From that steadiness, things begin to move. The quality of decisions improves, ownership expands as fear begins to fade and clarity takes the place of defensiveness. Stephen Covey did not say, "Seek first to interpret," or

"Seek first to fix," or even "to reframe." He said to understand, and to understand means being open to change. It asks you to listen in a way that allows what you hear to reshape the internal map you have been carrying.

That kind of moment is rare, but when it happens, it does more than help someone feel heard. It allows them to feel valued, not because they said the right thing or expressed themselves perfectly, but because they showed up fully and someone stayed with them through it. When people feel that kind of value, they begin to show up differently. They take more risks, let down their guard, and begin to lead in ways that feel honest.

The spaces between roles

Leadership helps set the tone, but culture is shaped in the spaces between roles. It takes root in how we relate to one another, not just in boardrooms or written values, but in the everyday moments between colleagues. It lives in the informal check-ins, the quick messages, and the quiet ways people either connect or miss one another across departments, titles, and temperaments.

Culture is not shaped by leaders alone. It is shaped by all of us, in the way we listen to one another across roles, across hierarchies, and within days already full of competing demands. Most teams do not struggle because they lack intelligence or motivation. They struggle because, at some point, they stop truly listening to each other.

This kind of breakdown rarely comes from neglect, and it is not usually caused by indifference. More often, it happens because people are stretched thin. Deadlines pile up, KPIs demand attention, and notifications interrupt focus, while the mental weight of too many priorities slowly takes its toll. In that kind of environment, communication turns transactional. It becomes brief, functional, and focused on output. Did you get the file? Are we aligned? Can this wait until next sprint? The pace is fast and efficient, but in the rush, something vital gets lost. It is the kind of listening that builds trust, the kind that allows people to feel seen as human beings rather than just roles to be filled.

Harvard researcher Amy Edmondson found that the highest-performing teams were not those made up of the smartest individuals, but those where people felt safe enough to take interpersonal risks. They felt able to ask a question, admit uncertainty, or offer a dissenting view without fearing damage to their reputation.[23] That kind of safety does not come from policy manuals. It comes from people who bring curiosity instead of preconceptions, and who listen not to reply but to understand. When that happens, when someone genuinely receives what another person is trying to share, the tension eases, the quality of attention shifts, and the conversation deepens.

Listening at work

I have seen teams move through weeks of creative stagnation not because they discovered the perfect framework, but because someone finally spoke the truth they had been holding back and someone else took the time to truly listen. Often it began with something small, a glance that said, *I noticed*, a well-timed question, or a quiet comment like, "You seemed hesitant. What is on your mind?" These gestures may seem minor, but they open doors that no formal process can reach.

Behind every agenda item and deliverable is a person wondering if they matter. Wondering if it is safe to admit they do not have the answer. Wondering if they can show up without having to pretend. When someone listens with patience, without rushing to fix or solve, the other person can begin to let go. Their shoulders ease, their voice steadies and they speak from somewhere closer to their centre. That is not weakness, it is what resilience in teams truly looks like.

Google's Project Aristotle pointed to the same truth: the most important factor in effective teams was not talent, structure, or clarity, but psychological safety.[24] At its heart are two quiet but radical questions: Do I feel heard, and do I feel safe to speak? These questions often draw the line between a group of professionals doing their jobs and a team that is able to think, take risks, and grow together.

Creating that kind of safety does not depend on a title, it begins with attention, not only to what is spoken but also to what is withheld. I have overlooked those moments myself, sometimes too focused on outcomes or moving too quickly to notice when someone needed more space.

Trust rarely breaks all at once. More often, it fades quietly, slipping away in the very moments when presence was needed but not offered.

I have also known the opposite, the moments when someone set their laptop aside, looked up from their phone, and said, "You went quiet. What is on your mind?" That kind of recognition changed everything, because I no longer needed to perform certainty or filter what I was feeling. I could speak freely, and in being met with undivided attention, the conversation was able to move into something more honest and more useful.

Listening is the bridge, and when enough people choose to cross it, meeting one another with attention instead of assumption, something begins to change. Culture does not shift through announcements or grand initiatives but through the quiet, repeated act of paying attention. When people feel heard, they do more than speak openly, they begin to care more deeply, invest more fully, and almost without effort, they learn to listen in return.

One call, everything changed

The first time I truly listened to a customer, I could feel his anger before he even finished saying hello, landing

Listening at work

like gravel, sharp and fast and unrelenting. He was not yelling just to make noise but because, in his experience, no one had been listening.

"You people sold me something that doesn't work," he said. "You told me it would be simple. You said it would help. Instead, it made everything worse."

At the time, I was running my SaaS business. It was a lean startup with a product we believed in, even as we continued to refine it. We had poured ourselves into its design, its architecture, and its promise to make life easier for horse trainers. And now one of those customers was on the phone, furious. This was not ordinary frustration, it was the kind of anger that is almost never about software.

For a moment, maybe three seconds, my whole system shifted into defense. I felt the urge to explain, to walk through the onboarding steps, to prove we were not the problem. But instead, almost without thinking, I said, "Hang on just a second." He stopped mid-sentence, caught off guard. "I want to grab a pen so I can write everything you say down."

There was a moment of silence, just a breath, but the shift was clear as his breathing slowed and his voice began to settle. He did not thank me or become friendly, yet something had changed. He realised I was present, not just as a company representative but as a person with a pen, ready to listen.

I did not explain or defend, nor did I promise to escalate or say I would take it under advisement. I simply wrote down what he said, line by line, frustration by frustration. Some of the issues turned out to be real bugs, while others were misunderstandings, but that was not the point. In that moment it did not matter who was right, what mattered was that he no longer felt alone with the problem.

We stayed on the phone for thirty minutes, maybe longer, and by the end the heat had lifted and his words no longer landed like shrapnel. He was thinking with me instead of pushing against me, and although we did not solve everything that day, something important had shifted.

Months went by as we continued to roll out updates, and I assumed I would not hear from him again. Then one morning, the phone rang and I recognised the voice immediately, but the tone had changed. He was not calling to complain, he was calling to say thank you.

"You probably don't remember me," he said.

"I do," I told him, smiling into the receiver.

"Well, I just wanted to say... your software didn't just help my business. It saved my marriage."

I went still, holding the phone as he explained that his wife had been helping with invoicing and admin. What began as a gesture of support had gradually become a source of strain, with late nights, frequent miscommunications, and the pressure of keeping everything afloat starting to spill into their relationship. They were arguing more, and resentment had begun to creep in, yet once the system started working for him and he understood how to use it, the tension eased. They stopped blaming each other, began sleeping better, and found themselves reconnecting in conversation and even laughing again.

I hadn't led a transformation or guided him through a rebrand, and I certainly hadn't overhauled his backend. All I had done was listen, staying with his anger without interrupting, without trying to explain or reframe, simply remaining present long enough for the fight to settle. Somehow, that changed everything.

In business, we talk constantly about customer experience. We map journeys, track satisfaction scores, measure retention, and analyse churn. We run user tests, refine onboarding flows, and even A/B test the colour of the Buy Now button. What we rarely create space for, though, is silence, the kind that allows someone to express their full frustration and still feel held. In those moments, the most powerful response is not *We're sorry you feel that way* or *Thanks for your understanding*, but simply *Tell me more*.

That is what real listening is. It is not a feature queue, not crisis management, and not reputation defence. It is honouring the humanity inside the frustration. Behind every angry email, cancelled account, or bad review is someone who trusted you with something that mattered, whether it was their time, their money, their hopes, their spouse's patience, or even their sense of worth. When that trust begins to fray, people do not need you to be perfect. They need you to stay with them in the unraveling.

Most businesses overlook this not because they do not care, but because listening can be uncomfortable, especially when the issue is not clean code or a simple fix. It is easier to argue, explain, or educate, yet people rarely remember whether they were wrong. What stays with them is whether they were heard. Sometimes, if you listen with enough stillness and without turning away, they will even call you back, not only to say the product is working but to tell you they feel whole again.

Part III: Deepening

Chapter 10.

Back to the beginning

There is a kind of listening that does not rely on words. It is not about nodding, paraphrasing or offering some variation of "what I'm hearing you say is...". It has nothing to do with technique. It is quieter than that, something felt more than performed, a presence that is full yet unobtrusive, rooted not in what you say but in how fully you are here.

I return to this kind of listening most often when I walk. Not the brisk walking I do for exercise and not the kind accompanied by a podcast or playlist, but the simple act of moving through space with nothing to solve and nothing to distract me.

Near my home in Melbourne there is a modest park. It is not wild or striking, just a few ovals of grass and a gravel path between residential streets. The trees are scattered, and the lawns are kept short by council crews for weekend sports and training nights. Families pass through on their way to school or errands, joggers trace the perimeter, children rattle past on bikes and dogs chase one another across the field with the seriousness of athletes in a finals match.

Most mornings the soundtrack is unremarkable, a voice carrying through a headset, the distant whine of a leaf blower, and the flute-like song of magpies, sometimes in duet, sometimes in a chorus.

When I stop, really stop, and settle onto one of the older benches near the back of the park, something inside me begins to loosen. The thoughts remain, circling as always. My mind replays half-finished tasks, unanswered emails, moments I wish I had handled differently, and quiet questions I have been avoiding. The noise is familiar, insistent, and for a while it holds on.

Gradually, another layer emerges beneath the churn. A breeze moves across my face, light as breath, while leaves shift overhead in a sound closer to a whisper than a rustle. Birds call and answer across the canopy, and an insect hums past as a bicycle glides over gravel somewhere nearby. Little by little, the thoughts lose their sharp edges, softening as the urgency begins to fade.

I do not fight the thoughts and I do not follow them. I let them pass and return each time to the quiet underneath. With time, a stillness appears, not something I create but something I remember, like stepping into a room I had not realised was open, a room I often forget is always there.

In that stillness I remember something important. I am not the voice in my head. I am the one hearing it, and that realisation changes everything. The part of me that

Back to the beginning

listens does not need to solve or interpret, and it does not even need to understand. It only needs to remain present.

When I do, something deeper rises. I remember that this listening is not new and not something I had to learn, because it has always been there. Long before language and long before comprehension, we knew how to listen. We attuned through breath and stillness, through the expressions in each other's eyes, feeling tone before we had words for emotion and reading the world through rhythm, posture, proximity, and the ancient intelligence of our bodies.

Babies still do this. Before they understand words, they listen with the full intensity of their being, responding to tone, to tempo, and to the quality of presence. They listen with their skin and their eyes, with every muscle resting in soft alertness.

That capacity does not vanish as we grow older. It becomes buried beneath layers of noise, both external and internal, in the meetings, the messages, the constant self-commentary, the pressure to prove or perform. Yet it never truly leaves.

When I sit in the park without trying to be present, when I release the effort and let awareness find me, that part of me stirs. It does not arrive with fanfare, but with the quiet certainty of something that has always been there. And for a while, I remember.

This is the original listening, not analysis or comprehension but something older and simpler, a felt sense of orientation, attunement, and belonging, a way of knowing that does not need thought to be true.

And when I find my way back to it, I cannot help but wonder how we lost it. If this is how we once listened, instinctively, bodily, and without effort, what was it that pulled us away? How did something so natural become so rare, and how did we grow fluent in expressing ourselves yet hesitant when it comes to receiving each other fully?

That is where this chapter begins, not with advice or technique but with return, a slow walk back through the history of listening, not as data or skill but as inheritance. Listening began not with dialogue but with breath, with the body, and with the silence beneath the trees, and perhaps the way forward is to begin there again.

I sometimes imagine the earliest humans, not as stiff figures frozen in museum dioramas, but as real people who lived without electricity or clocks, without the buzz of traffic or the glow of screens that now shapes so much of our experience. They moved through their days by firelight and measured time by the shifting sun. When the labour of survival was done, they did not search for something to fill the silence. They listened.

They listened not to learn, to be entertained, or to win an argument, but because their lives depended on it. They listened to the wind and what its change in direction might mean, to the brittle snap of movement through dry undergrowth, to the call and reply of birds overhead, and to the sudden stillness that signalled a coming storm. Listening was not a luxury or a virtue, it was how they stayed alive.

Long before writing, people began to listen to each other. Before language took a fixed form, meaning passed between them through a hand resting gently on the chest, the rhythm of breath, a subtle tightening of the shoulders, or a shift in gaze that spoke more than words ever could. The earliest stories were not told as we tell them now. They were felt as much as spoken, carried in gesture, tone, silence, movement, and presence.

One person would share what they had seen, whether it was a hunt, a danger, a dream, or a death. Another would receive it without critique or commentary, only stillness and widened eyes. These early listeners were not skilled in argument or persuasion. They were simply available, and that deep, receptive presence gave rise to something else. It became memory.

Story came before scrolls, books, or data storage. It was not story for entertainment, but story as archive, a living continuity passed from mouth to ear and shaped as much by cadence as by content. In oral traditions, the rhythm, tone, and melody of a voice are not decoration, they are the vessel. In many cultures, meaning was co-created in the space between speaker and listener, and a story was not complete until it had been received and allowed to settle. As some Indigenous communities say, "The story belongs to the listener now."

That idea reframes listening as stewardship. To listen in this way is to honour what has been given and to join something larger than yourself, not only as a witness but as a keeper of memory. Across time, cultures, and spiritual traditions, there is the same reverence for listening, not as absence but as practice. In monastic life, silence becomes devotion. Monks who take vows of silence are not withdrawing from life, they are listening more deeply to it. Quakers gather in silence not because they have nothing to say, but because they are waiting for something truer to emerge. In the Torah, the first instruction from God is not to obey, follow, or speak. It is to listen. *Shema Yisrael*. Hear, O Israel. Not interpret, not analyse, just hear.

Buddhists speak of deep listening. Christians speak of discernment. Sufis speak of sama, a listening that opens the soul to the sacred. Over time, as the pace of life quickened and the world tilted toward output and efficiency, we began to forget. We started treating listening as something passive, a pause between the parts that mattered, a polite intermission before returning to contributing, clarifying, and responding. Yet for most of human history, listening was never a break in the action, it was the action. It was the thread that connected experience to understanding, the bridge between individual awareness and collective meaning. It was how we survived, how we bonded, and how we came to know the world, not in isolation but together.

Back to the beginning

Sacred listening across traditions

Across cultures and centuries, listening has never been just a means of communication. It has been a spiritual practice, valued not for its outcomes but for the space it creates. In many traditions, it is understood as a form of prayer. Long before modern psychology introduced words like attunement or presence, spiritual communities were already centering their lives around the quiet strength of receptive attention.

In early Christianity, silence and listening formed the ground of contemplative life. The Desert Fathers, monks who retreated into the wilderness during the third and fourth centuries, sought stillness not as an escape from the world but as a way to prepare for something deeper. They listened for what they called the small, still voice, believing that divine truth did not arrive with force. It had to be sensed, awaited, and received.

In Buddhist teaching, the practice of deep listening, known as *shravana* in Sanskrit, is understood as a path to liberation. Thích Nhất Hạnh described it as an act of compassion. To listen fully to another's suffering, without judgment, without interruption, and without the need to fix, becomes a form of healing in itself. In Islam, particularly within Sufi mysticism, sacred listening takes form through *sama*, a spiritual practice that draws on music, poetry, and chant to create a space for divine connection. These are not performances to be analyzed. They are portals, meant to be received so deeply that the sound settles inside you and something within begins to shift.

In Indigenous cultures, where oral tradition came long before writing, listening was seen as a sign of wisdom. Elders did more than pass down stories, they watched closely to see how those stories were received, because what could be shared was not only knowledge but also the ability to carry it with care. In the Quaker tradition, this same reverence for listening shapes the gathering itself, where worship begins not with a sermon but with silence. A room of people listens, not for their own thoughts, but for what Quakers call the Inner Light, and sometimes someone speaks, moved by what they hear within, while at other times no one does. In either case, the silence is not empty, it is sacred.

Across these traditions, a shared understanding begins to surface. Truth does not always come through language. Sometimes it arrives through space, and that space begins with listening, the kind that loosens its hold on certainty and allows something sacred to enter. This may arise in the other, within oneself, or in the quiet space between. Some traditions gave it structure, while others passed it on through presence and example, but the message remained the same. To listen with depth is to take part in something larger than yourself, something both ancient and alive.

That reverence is not limited to monasteries or meditation halls. In Japan, it can be found in everyday life. The word *haragei* (腹芸), which means "belly art," refers to a kind of intuitive communication that happens beneath the surface. It is not expressed through argument or explanation, but through shared presence. You listen to what is said and to what is left unsaid. The pauses, the breath, the tilt of a head, or the softening of someone's eyes all carry meaning. In traditional Japanese aesthetics, silence is not empty. It is full. The word *ma* (間) captures this quality, the space that exists between things. It appears in music, in architecture, and in conversation. In many Western cultures, silence is seen as a gap, something that needs to be filled. In Japan, it can be a gift. It becomes a sign of respect, an offering of space where another's words can truly land.

Even the structure of the Japanese language reflects this way of being. Subjects are often left unspoken because they are already understood. The words for "I" and "you" quietly recede, allowing context to carry the meaning. Listening is not only valued, it is woven into the language itself. This does not mean Japanese culture is without conflict or noise. It means that deep, embodied listening is practiced not only in sacred spaces, but also in the rhythm of daily life.

In Aikido, everything begins with connection. I did not realise it at the time, but through the training I was learning *haragei*, the art of listening beneath language, a way of sensing what someone is about to do before they do it, not through guessing but through attunement. This kind of listening is not passive, it is fully engaged even when it appears still, and responsive even when no words are spoken.

Like so many ancient ways of knowing, it is easy to forget. Not because it has lost its value, but because the world has grown louder, faster, and more distracted. You can find it in the silence before a bow, in the way one person slows their breath to meet another's, in the pause between question and answer, and in the quiet understanding that sometimes the most truthful response is no response at all.

How the world understood listening

For a long time, I saw philosophy as something abstract, an intellectual pursuit that lived in lecture halls or under olive trees. It seemed full of thought experiments and dense arguments. I pictured men in robes or tweed jackets, pacing and pontificating, their heads filled with ideas and their mouths rarely still. But the more I listened, the more I began to notice something quieter. The wisest philosophers were not always the ones who spoke the most. They were the ones who listened most deeply.

Take Socrates. We remember him through his questions, through the method that still carries his name. He walked the streets of Athens, drawing people into conversation not to win, but to understand. At its core, his method was not built on argument, it was rooted in inquiry. He listened not just to what people said, but to what lived beneath their words. The assumptions they had never examined. The contradictions they held without realizing. He listened for the edge, the place where someone's thinking met the limit of what they had ever spoken aloud, and when he reached that place, he did not use it to shame or defeat, he used it to help them see. Socrates knew that real freedom does not come from being given the truth, it comes from finding it yourself, often through struggle, through dialogue, and in the presence of someone who is truly listening.

Centuries later, in another part of the world and within a very different tradition, the Buddha offered something strikingly similar. In the Pali canon, there is a teaching called *kalyāṇa-mitta*, which means spiritual friendship, the simple but radical idea that awakening does not happen in isolation but requires companionship. This companionship is not found in gurus or fixers but in fellow travellers who walk beside us, people who can sit with our pain without trying to erase it, who can hold space without needing to solve anything. In this tradition, listening is not separate from enlightenment but is part of the path itself.

The Stoics, though less direct, understood this as well and wrote often about perception, attention, and the practice of inner stillness. Epictetus, once enslaved, is remembered for saying, "We have two ears and one mouth so that we can listen twice as much as we speak." Taken seriously, this is more than common sense, it is a quiet reordering of priorities. To live this way means your first responsibility in a conversation is not to be understood but to understand, which does not require disappearing or agreeing with everything you hear. It requires slowing down, loosening the grip on being right, and making space for something greater than your own certainty. For the Stoics, listening was a form of temperance, a kind of humility that asked whether the picture might be incomplete, whether something important had not yet been heard.

In the twentieth century, the Austrian psychologist Alfred Adler, one of the lesser-known founders of modern therapy, brought these ideas into the emotional realm. He believed that much of human suffering arose from disconnection, from the sense of not being seen, of not mattering, of feeling invisible in the presence of others. To address that, he did not turn to diagnosis or theory but instead offered presence. Adler's approach was deeply relational, grounded in the belief that the task of the therapist, and perhaps the task of any human being, was not to interpret or advise but to understand the world from within another person's experience. He called this social interest, a form of empathy rooted in our shared human condition.

Later, Carl Rogers would call it unconditional positive regard, and Marshall Rosenberg would describe it as empathic connection. To me, it is a way of listening that takes in the whole person, not just the words they speak but also the feeling beneath them, the emotions they have not named, the weight they did not mean to share but carried in with them, and the things for which they have no words yet still bring forward between the lines.

When you step back across time, across cultures, and across traditions, a pattern begins to emerge. From

Back to the beginning

Athens to India, from the forests of early Buddhism to Stoic Rome to Viennese clinics, there is a quiet agreement that listening is not what happens while you wait to speak, and it is not a performance or a technique. It is a way of being, carried in your breath, shaped in the pause, and known in the space between words.

The erosion of listening in modern culture

Somewhere along the way, we stopped listening. It didn't happen all at once, and it wasn't deliberate. It unfolded gradually, like a shoreline shaped by tide after tide. Each wave seemed small on its own, yet over time, it redrew the entire edge of our attention. Stillness gave way to speed. Pauses to productivity. And conversation, once a space for presence and connection, began to drift into something more performative.

We began to treat communication as a contest. We wanted to be right, to sound sharper, to deliver the most compelling take in the least amount of time. We learned to speak in soundbites, to brand our thoughts, and to compress our feelings into something legible, likable, and quick. Instead of reflecting, we reacted. Instead of attuning, we advised. Instead of staying, we scrolled.

Even in spaces created for connection, such as dinner tables, classrooms, and therapy rooms, the pace has quickened. People are multitasking, managing, distracted, and often only partly present. Where attention was once given freely, it now feels scattered, conditional, or held back. We may still speak with fluency, but we have become unpractised in presence.

The loss is quiet, but its effects are unmistakable. You can feel it in conversations that drift without landing, in moments when something tender is shared and met not with care, but with quick commentary. You notice it when someone responds too fast, too clever, too soon, before your words have had time to settle. And you recognise it in the ache that follows, the one that whispers as you walk away. *They didn't really hear me.*

That quiet ache is all around us. It shows up in relationships that struggle to find their rhythm, in workplaces where teams speak often but rarely connect, and in public discourse that moves too quickly to hold much meaning. It feels sharp, reactive, and fragile. You see it in children who stop sharing. Not because they have nothing to say, but because no one listens beyond their behaviour.

And if you are paying attention, you will feel it in yourself. In the urge to fill silence, in the need to soften discomfort, or in the impulse to start forming a reply before the other person has even finished speaking. In the quiet panic that rises when a moment lingers too long without resolution. And in the reflex to act, to shift, to do anything other than stay.

Back to the beginning

But this does not mean something is beyond repair. It simply means we are underpractised. Most of us were never taught how to listen in a world like this. One filled with constant alerts, curated identities, and scattered attention, where time feels limited and presence even more so.

The capacity to listen has not disappeared. It is still here, just beneath the surface. Beneath the reflex to react, the pace of daily life, and the endless scroll. Like stars hidden behind city lights, it remains unchanged. Listening waits for us to pause, to soften our grip, to remember what we have always known.

Chapter 11.

How listening changes relationships

Bang. No warning. No countdown. A trigger pulled and it is off, like Usain Bolt out of the blocks but with more heat than grace.

Sometimes it starts small, a cup left by the sink or shoes scattered in the hallway as if someone shed the day without noticing. Other times it is not small at all, such as a hard meeting, the boys dodging chores or the invisible weight of one too many things finally tipping over. Whatever the spark, I can sense it in Antoinette before I can explain it. Her voice sharpens, her movements become quick and decisive, and her eyes lock in with that fierce, familiar focus. She talks faster, reaches for tasks, starts cleaning or organizing with sudden urgency, not rage exactly but something older, a frantic urgency trying to outrun a weight that has no name.

I used to meet it with logic. I would rewind the moment, gather the evidence and ask myself if it was something I said, something the boys did not do or something I had missed. I spoke softly and carefully, trying to slow things down, offer reasons, create space and reframe the tone. What I called clarity, she felt as gaslighting. I understand that now.

I was not trying to hurt her. I was trying to manage the moment, to soothe it, explain it and pull it back toward calm. I believed that if I could find the right words she would land and we could reset. Yet even my soft words, especially the ones shaped with logic and distance, felt like ice rather than balm.

Eventually I began to see it. This was not about the dishes, the boys or even about me. This was pain, old pain, the kind that does not ask to be solved but only to be seen. History was flooding through the body, a nervous system hijacked, a thousand past moments compressed into this one and spilling through the cracks. And I was trying to talk it down, but you cannot reason with what someone's body remembers.

So now, when I catch it in time, I do not meet it with defense. I do not explain, argue facts or offer perspective. I listen, not only to the words but to what is trembling underneath them, the desperation, the disorientation and the deep cry for something to feel safe. I slow my breath, soften my gaze and stay close, not intrusive and not retreating, just present.

And slowly, sometimes so slowly you would miss it if you were not paying attention, she begins to return. Her voice loses its edge, her eyes find mine and her body starts to remember the ground beneath her. Here is what I have come to know. I used to think that staying silent

How listening changes relationships

meant giving in. Now I understand it is a kind of strength.

This was not something I figured out on my own. At some point I began listening in other directions as well, not only to my partner or my breath but to the research. I was not reading in an academic way, more like following a breadcrumb trail that kept affirming what my body already sensed before my mind could explain it.

Gottman spent decades studying couples in detail. In his lab, partners were wired up, heart rates monitored, facial expressions tracked and stress responses recorded as they talked, argued, laughed or simply sat in silence. What he found was surprisingly simple. Relationships did not last because there was no conflict, they lasted because of how couples moved through it. The ones who stayed present in the heat of discomfort and turned toward each other instead of away, not only physically but also emotionally, were the ones who endured. They did not avoid storms, they learned how to stay anchored inside them.

Even their bodies told the story. Partners in connected relationships had healthier immune systems, as if their nervous systems could tell when they were being held rather than hurt. But when defensiveness set in, when one or both partners shut down, lashed out or withdrew, everything shifted. Cortisol surged, heart rates jumped and listening collapsed. What began as a disagreement became something more primal, a physiological threat not to an idea but to the person.

I know that pattern, the quickening breath, the tightening chest, the moment when feeling misunderstood turns into an impulse not to listen but to push back, to correct and to defend. What I keep learning, slowly and imperfectly, is that staying with someone's experience does not mean abandoning your own. It does not mean collapsing or conceding, and it does not mean they are right and you are wrong. It means choosing connection over control and presence over power.

It means resisting the urge to fix and becoming the kind of presence where what is broken does not need to be hidden. More than anything, that is what shifts the ground between people. It is not about solving the pain but about showing up so it does not have to carry itself alone. That is the kind of partner I am trying to become, not the fixer, not the analyst, not the one who always knows what to say, but someone who stays steady, attuned and fully there.

Why we harden

Most people do not raise their voices simply to be loud, they raise them because they do not feel heard. When they fall silent it is rarely a sign of peace. More often it is a form of protest or resignation, a nervous system pulling back not out of grace but from sheer exhaustion.

It took me a long time to recognise this. For years I believed I was the calm one, the steady voice in the storm. I did not yell or accuse, I stayed measured and rational, and I thought that was enough. I assumed it meant I was safe to be around.

Over time I learned that restraint does not always mean safety. You can sit still and speak gently while broadcasting judgment so loudly it fills the room. You can wrap tension in politeness and use a soft voice while sending the message, hurry up, calm down, get back to normal. People sense it. Even if they cannot name what is happening, they feel it in their bodies.

That is why people harden. Something in them doesn't feel safe enough to soften. Real safety, the kind that allows someone to stay present when their instinct is to shut down, does not come from niceness. It comes from the nervous system.

Shut Up – A journey into the lost art of listening

I'd learned this first with my son, watching him freeze before his exam. His body knew something his mind couldn't articulate. The same pattern played out on the mat in Aikido, where a tense partner's grip would telegraph their fear before they moved. And now I was seeing it everywhere, in Antoinette's voice when it went tight, in the way colleagues would shut down mid-meeting, in my own chest when criticism landed sideways.

The body is always listening, always scanning. Not consciously, but constantly. It reads the room faster than thought, registering whether this moment, this person, this conversation feels safe. And when it decides the answer is no, when the signals don't align, when someone's calm words carry an undertone of judgment or their patience feels like barely contained frustration, the system doesn't wait for proof. It reacts.

We brace. We deflect. We go quiet or we go loud. Not because we're broken, but because we're wired for survival.

Real listening offers the opposite of that alarm. It sends a signal beneath language that says you don't need your armor here. You can put down the sword. And when the body receives that message, truly receives it and believes it, something shifts. The breath deepens. The shoulders drop. The grip loosens. Not because anything has been solved, but because for the first time in that moment, we're not alone with it.

What lets us soften

When someone I loved was in pain, I thought my job was to help them make sense of it. I would reframe the moment, give it structure and offer a perspective they could use. With those closest to me, I wanted to help, to steady them, soothe the ache and offer something that might restore balance.

What I did not realise was how often I was rushing. It was not because I did not care but because I was uncomfortable. Their pain stirred something in me I did not yet know how to hold, and without meaning to, I tried to make it smaller, not only for them but also for me.

When someone feels rushed, even in the subtlest ways, when their pain is interrupted, redirected or reframed too soon, they rarely feel supported. They feel managed, and something begins to close. The trust that allowed them to speak in the first place starts to contract.

I have felt that contraction in my own body. You say something tender, uncertain and still forming, and the reply comes too quickly. It might be a suggestion, a silver lining or an insight meant to help, and maybe it is helpful, but it does not land that way. It lands like a door closing before you have stepped through, like being asked to move on before you have even arrived.

So you close, not in anger and not always with awareness, but in a quiet, protective way. Your words come more slowly, your openings grow smaller and you move as if carrying something fragile.

The irony is that we do this to each other without meaning to. We are not trying to shut anyone down, we are trying to connect, but in a way the body does not trust. The body does not open in response to insight, it opens in response to presence.

What helps people soften is not what we say but what we signal. We show that we are here, that we are not afraid of what they are carrying and that they do not have to shrink it to make it easier for us to hold. When that message is clear, the door opens. Breath deepens, shoulders drop and the voice slows, not because something has been resolved but because it no longer needs to be performed. The nervous system begins to settle and quietly returns home.

It rarely looks dramatic and there is no sudden breakthrough or emotional flood, only the subtle feeling of someone returning to themselves. I have seen it happen in seconds. Someone walks in braced, ready for conflict, and instead meets acceptance. Not analysis, not reassurance, not advice, only the quiet steadiness of someone who will not look away.

I see you. I am not flinching. I can hold this.

And something lets go, not out of surrender and not out of defeat, but because for the first time the nervous system believes it can put its sword down.

How listening changes relationships

When I reflect on what truly helps people soften and allows truth to unfold rather than brace itself for defence, it has never been the words I found that mattered most. It was that I stopped needing to find them. I let the silence be safe, let the pain be welcome and let the truth remain unedited. That, more than insight or timing or anything I might have said, is what allows someone to feel held, not because I said the right thing but because I stopped trying so hard to prove I knew what it was.

A mountain to climb

When my eldest son turned fifteen, I took him on a trip to Far North Queensland. It was just the two of us with no siblings, no partners and no distractions, only time, space and open sky.

I wanted it to be more than a holiday. In many tribal cultures, boys go through initiation, a clear and embodied threshold that marks the moment they are no longer children. That moment matters not only for the boy but also for the father. This was my way of giving him something like that, a modern version of a rite of passage.

We filled the week with adventure. We went tree surfing, took crocodile tours, raced go-karts and discovered hidden waterholes. We also spent a few nights at a yoga and meditation retreat tucked into the green folds of the hills, where the air felt softer, silence was welcomed and time seemed to slow its breath. I wanted him to feel not only the rush of thrill but also the weightless calm of stillness, the pull of introspection and the quiet understanding that strength does not always look like dominance.

The part I had been planning for months was the test. It was not about toughness or survival, but about meeting something deeper, a part of himself he might not have met before. The mountain would ask for his patience, his focus and his resolve. He would lead me up Mount Sorrow.

The trailhead was almost hidden, marked by a small sign half-covered by bush. We set out early, the tropical humidity already clinging to our skin. The climb was steep and unrelenting, with roots coiling across the path so we had to scramble over them using both hands and feet. The forest floor was damp and rich with decay, and each step felt alive beneath us. Snakes slipped off the path just ahead, their movement vanishing into the undergrowth. We paused for water but never for long.

About a hundred metres from the top, the air cooled and mist began to wrap around us. We were climbing into cloud and into a quiet that felt as if it belonged to another altitude. The trees thinned, the temperature dropped and patches of sky opened through the canopy. We could not yet see the summit, but the air carried a different weight. The trail grew brighter and we knew we were close.

I turned to him and said, "Go on ahead. Finish the last stretch on your own. Take a moment at the top and think about what you have just done and what it means." He nodded, took a breath and walked on without looking back. I stood watching him, this boy I had raised, moving with steady determination through the mist. Then I let him go.

Five minutes later I followed. At the top, he was already standing on the small aluminium platform, its surface pale and raw against the sky, carried up piece by piece through the heart of the bush. The clouds floated below us, and beyond them the land and sea unfurled in quiet layers. The forest folded into the coastline, the coastline softened into the silver horizon, and for a moment the whole world seemed to hold its breath.

We stood side by side without speaking. There was nothing to explain and nothing to narrate. We had done something hard, both together and apart. He had led, and I was no longer the only one who needed to lead.

As I write this I am preparing for another journey, this time with my youngest son. We are heading to Bali, a place of lush contours and slower time, where the world feels less digitised and more elemental. The landscape will be different, the language unfamiliar and the pace unhurried in the best possible way. Yet the purpose at its core remains the same.

Like the trip I took years ago with his brother, this is a quiet invitation. It is a chance to step away from the momentum of everyday life and into something more spacious, something that does not ask him to perform or explain but simply to be. I want to give him time to stretch into himself, to meet challenge and beauty without commentary, and to sense in his own way that something inside him is beginning to shift.

He is a different boy, shaped by his own rhythms, his own sensibilities and his own way of moving through the world. Where his older brother is relaxed and open to trying new things, this one holds his cards closer. He notices what others miss but rarely speaks of it, his sensitivity running deep and often shielded by humour or distraction. I want to honour that. I want him to feel, without being told, that becoming himself does not need to follow anyone else's pace.

I do not know what his mountain will be, in either the literal or symbolic sense, and I do not need to. I trust we will recognise it when it appears. Some threshold will emerge, subtle yet unmistakable, and when it does I will step aside. I will give him the lead not because I am pulling back but because I want him to feel the shape of his own agency, the weight of his own choices and the quiet strength of being trusted. He will not need to prove anything, only to arrive, and I will be there.

When the moment comes, I will wait for him on the other side. There will be no answers offered and no fanfare, only the steady presence I have learned to give when words are not what is needed. I will not rush to name the moment or draw meaning from it, but will remain steady and available, letting the silence speak for itself.

Some things are best understood not through dialogue but through the quiet of shared experience. And sometimes the most enduring way to say I see you is not with words at all, but by standing beside someone, unhurried and open, until they find their way up their mountain.

Chapter 12.

Listening to Yourself

It began with something small, insignificant by most standards, yet sharp in its quiet way.

I was in the kitchen, barefoot, standing over a sink of dishes while the kettle clicked off. In the next room, my boys were playing with their Beyblades, mid-argument over which one was the strongest. Their voices rose and fell in the rhythm of competition, part play and part conviction. One of them narrated under his breath, lost in a world of spinning tops, imagined powers and battle cries.

Inside me, everything felt wrong. It was not dramatic, but it wrapped around me completely. A heaviness in my limbs. A pressure behind my eyes. The feeling you get when you've been holding your breath without realizing it, and your whole body is waiting for permission to exhale. It was the kind of wrongness that appears when nothing is wrong, yet somehow everything is.

I exhaled and realised I had been holding my breath. It was not a sigh, only a slow leak that brought no relief, just the awareness of how long I had been clenched.

Then I heard it. Not out loud, but clear enough to stop me mid-motion, my hand frozen over the next dish.

Come on. You're fine. Just get it done.

The voice was not harsh or angry. It was quiet and steady, a kind of command that moved through emotion without pause. It was firm and efficient, never asking questions, always getting things done.

Without thinking, I obeyed. I rinsed the cup and reached for the next one in a single, practiced motion. Yet somewhere inside, something faltered. It was small, almost invisible, like a ripple across still water. That voice, that quiet instruction, made me wonder who it was for, and who it might be silencing.

I had always believed I had a good relationship with myself. I wasn't harsh or cruel. I made time to reflect and to grow, journaling enough to feel connected. I thought I was listening.

Over time, I began to see that I wasn't really listening to myself at all. I was managing, directing, and coaching my way through each moment as if life were a task needing constant supervision. When something tender rose, whether it was grief, doubt, or loneliness, I did not meet it with curiosity. I met it with commentary.

Listening to Yourself

It's not a big deal. Other people have it worse. You're probably just tired.

On the surface, these thoughts seemed responsible, yet beneath them was a habit of silencing the parts of me that spoke too softly to be convenient.

It was as though there were two versions of me. One moved slowly, still trying to understand what it felt. The other was fast, composed, and always ready with a rational explanation. The fast one often took over, smoothing discomfort before I had the chance to sit with it. It kept life neat and safe, but it also shut down the part of me that most needed to be heard.

I began to wonder what would happen if I did not interrupt myself. If I stopped narrating and simply listened without reframing or fixing. Could I give myself the same attention I was trying to give others, with patience, tenderness and space to exist?

That day, nothing outwardly changed. I finished the dishes, made the tea, and sat at the table like always. But inside, something shifted. It was a quiet sense that something was off. I felt tight, as though I was holding something back, and instead of brushing it away, I stayed.

I stayed with the sensation, not to understand or solve it, but simply to acknowledge it. I closed my eyes because the room had grown too loud. I placed a hand on my chest because my body asked for it. There was heat, but no pain, only a rawness, as if something had been worn thin.

Then I heard it. Not a thought, but a whisper from somewhere deeper.

I'm tired of pretending I'm okay.

It rose from my body like a lump in the throat. Out of habit, I almost dismissed it. Of course you're tired, everyone's tired, you're fine. But for once, I let it stay.

I'm tired of pretending I'm okay.

The words landed differently the second time. Heavier. Truer. It was not clarity or relief, but permission. Permission to not know why, to feel heavy without needing to justify it, to sit at the table with no answers and still belong.

That was the first time I understood what it meant to listen inward, not as a strategy but as an act of awareness. I was beginning to offer myself the same space I offered others, even to the parts that had no words.

And in that small, unresolved moment, with nothing explained, I felt more whole than I had in weeks. Not because I understood anything new, but because I had not talked over myself. I had stayed and I had listened, and something long-overlooked in me felt met.

Stillness as self-attunement

I did not become a teacher because I was ready, or even because I wanted to. It happened because one afternoon the phone rang and Sensei's voice came through, calm and certain. "You're up," he said.

There was no warning. No slow lead-in. Just a short call delivered with the kind of quiet authority you do not argue with.

He had moved to Canberra a few years before, part of his own deepening, though he never put it into words. In his absence, Daniel, the most senior student, had been holding the classes. Now Daniel was leaving for New York, and someone had to take his place.

That someone, it turned out, was me.

"Let me know if you need anything," Sensei said. "I'll come back on weekends when I can. Teach what you need to learn." Then the line went silent.

No syllabus, no orientation, no chance to ease into the role. Only a passing of responsibility so quiet it almost felt like nothing had changed. Yet everything had.

You're up. Figure it out.

That first night I arrived early, as I always did. Gi and hakama already on, belt tied, my body doing its best to act like it knew what it was doing. I unlocked the dojo, an old hall no longer used by the scouts, and stepped into the stillness. There was the familiar scent of dust and old timber, the soft creak of floorboards, and the hush that always made it feel as though something sacred was about to begin.

I picked up the mop and began to clean the floor, not out of obligation but instinct. It was my way of arriving, of settling into the space, of remembering what mattered. When I finished, I laid out the mats, smoothing the seams and checking the corners as though tending to an altar. I had no idea how many people would come, whether none, one, or more. Still, I moved through the rhythm as I always had, preparing the space and listening for whatever might show up.

Eventually, they arrived, familiar faces I had trained beside for years. They bowed at the door, smiled, and made quiet conversation as they stretched. No one mentioned the change, and no one needed to. I could feel it in the air, the subtle edge that comes when you are the one standing at the front.

When it was time, I walked to the shomen, checked that everything was in place, and knelt in silence. Two bows. Two claps. One final bow. Then I turned to face the class and bowed again."*Onegaishimas (*お願いします*).* "They bowed in return."*Onegaishimas."*

Onegaishimas is a hard phrase to translate. Technically, it means something like "I humbly request," yet in the dojo it carries more weight. It says I entrust myself to you. Let us train sincerely, together. It is a mutual offering, a quiet contract of respect.

And just like that, I was teaching.

I was nervous. I could feel it in the height of my breath and the faint stiffness across my shoulders, but I knew where to begin. We always started with the same technique, *tai no henko*, one I had practiced a thousand times or more. It lived in the bones, a foundational movement, simple in form yet deep in practice, turning from the center, blending with the energy, extending ki. There was no flourish and nothing to perform, only the quiet rhythm of being.

The moment we began, everything else fell away as my breath settled and my body remembered. The mental chatter receded like a tide and I dropped into that quiet state, not thinking but listening, moving, responding and leading from the body.

I remembered something Sensei had told me once, when I asked how you know you are ready to teach. "The students are there for the teacher," he said. "Teach what you need to learn."

That stayed with me.

So that is what I did. I did not try to impress anyone or prove anything, only to begin with what grounded me, what I needed to remember, the feeling of center, of connection, of flow. Somehow, that was enough.

The class unfolded without effort, technique to technique, not from a plan but from presence. I watched their bodies and felt the room, noticing the subtle shifts as a shoulder tensed, a gaze drifted or a posture softened, and I let those cues guide what came next. I was not performing or proving anything, only practicing, in public.

That night, I came to understand something I had not fully grasped before. Teaching is not about what you know. It is about how you show up, how your nervous system speaks long before your words do. It is in your presence, your pacing, and your ability to stay grounded in yourself while holding space for someone else. That kind of presence does not come from expertise or control. It comes from listening, not just with your ears but with your whole body, to what is here in this moment. That is what *tai no henko* teaches you. It is what the mat teaches you. It is what I keep learning each time I bow in, sweep the floor, and say, "*Onegaishimas.*"

Self-awareness had always felt like an anchor, something I valued and tried to live by. Not the curated kind shaped for confession or performance, with no public reckonings and no tidy apologies shared over cocktails or posted online. I mean the quiet kind, internal and unseen, where you pay attention, reflect and own your part. If something felt off, whether in a conversation or on the mat, I would replay it afterward, scanning for

Listening to Yourself

what I had missed, what I could have done better and where I had failed to fully show up. That process felt like growth, a sign of integrity and a way of taking responsibility.

It took years to realize that what I called awareness was often judgment in a better outfit. It did not sound like blame, it sounded like standards and discipline, the voice of a wise inner coach who wanted me to do better. Yet beneath that language, neat and deceptively helpful, was something tighter and more anxious. It was not trying to understand me but to correct me, slipping in quietly through the ordinary rather than arriving with drama. I would say something in a meeting and immediately hear, *Why did you say it that way?* I would walk away from a conversation with my partner and think, *You talked too much again.* I would stand at the edge of the mat watching students and hear, *You are not fully grounded, they can feel that, get it together.* It was not cruel, just constant, like a background narrator with a red pen.

For a long time, I thought this vigilance was what growth required, a kind of ruthless self-honesty that noticed every flaw before someone else could. But over time I began to see that this voice was not curious, it did not want to learn. It was defensive, scanning for threat, trying to stay ahead of failure and avoid rejection by correcting myself before anyone else had the chance. That was not awareness. It was bracing.

In Nonviolent Communication there is a distinction between observation and evaluation that stayed with me from the first time I heard it. Observation is neutral and grounded, simply describing what is there. Evaluation is loaded. It carries interpretation, assumption, and often a quiet layer of shame. Observation might say, "I spoke for 80% of that conversation." Evaluation turns it into, "I dominated the conversation again. Why can't I just listen?" Observation notices, "My body feels tense right now." Evaluation concludes, "I am too reactive. I need to calm down." One creates space. The other closes it.

I began to wonder what might shift if I stopped evaluating myself and simply observed. Not as a strategy for improvement or a subtler form of control, but as a way of being with myself. Not as a project to fix, but as a person to meet. I started small, with quiet experiments in noticing. When I caught the judgmental voice rising, I would pause, not to silence it but to acknowledge it gently. I named it with a soft internal nod, *"Ah, there you are."* Then I would shift the question from *What is wrong with me?* to *What is happening here?*

Sometimes that meant sitting on the edge of the mat after class, simply feeling the exhaustion in my body without turning it into a story. Sometimes it meant catching a spiral mid-thought and letting *"I am such an idiot"* soften into *"I feel embarrassed."* That subtle shift began to change everything. When I stopped judging myself for being reactive, I noticed I became less reactive. When I stopped shaming myself for drifting, I found I could return to presence. And when I stopped using awareness as a form of self-surveillance, it softened into something else entirely.

Compassion.

It sounds gentle, but it is not soft in the way people imagine. It is the voice that says, *You are learning, this is hard, and that's ok, you still belong here.* Even now, I do not always get it right. The judgment still comes, quick and practiced. But I am quicker to recognise it for what it is, fear dressed up as discipline. And when I can meet that fear with breath instead of critique, I return to something quieter. Something that feels less like correction and more like an internal bow.

Plenty of time

I once gave myself an entire day without time. Antoinette was away, and the boys were with their mum. There were no meetings, no deadlines, and nothing to measure the hours, no clocks, no screens, no devices quietly reminding me where I was in the day. Just me, alone, with no markers except the light in the sky and the rhythm of my own attention.

The night before, I covered every clock, unplugged my devices, and removed anything that might pull me back into my usual rhythm. I wanted to clear away all the cues that kept me tuned to the world outside so I could tune into the quieter one inside.

Shut Up – A journey into the lost art of listening

Morning came overcast and without the sun to orient me, the hours dissolved into one another. I had no way of knowing if it was mid-morning or late afternoon, and for once, that felt like a relief.

I moved slowly through the day, with yoga, Qi Gong, and meditation. I walked the length of my home with no destination except to notice what I noticed. These practices, so often pushed to the edges of my week, now had no end point and no quiet declaration of "enough for today."

In the stillness I began to hear myself more clearly. At first it was only the familiar noise I carry, the planning voice, the critic and the endless list-maker. As the hours unfolded, other voices began to surface, ones that rarely find space over the rush. I heard what my body had been trying to tell me about fatigue, the edges of questions I had been avoiding, and a longing for something slower, not as a break but as a way of living.

I sat with my bonsai tree, tracing the lines of its bark and letting its stillness steady mine. Later I turned over an hourglass and watched the sand fall, noticing the patterns it formed and the way it kept its own pace regardless of mine. The irony was not lost on me that I was learning to listen by ignoring the very thing the hourglass measured.

As the day went on my mind began to loosen. I realised I had spent years asking others to listen more deeply to each other, to what is unspoken and to what lives beneath the words, without noticing how rarely I had offered that same attention to myself.

Listening to Yourself

Listening to yourself is not the same as thinking about yourself. It is not turning over the same worries or replaying the same stories. It is meeting what is present without judgment, without rushing to fix or explain. It is the same discipline we practise when we offer presence to someone else, only turned toward our own inner voice.

By the time night arrived, and I only knew it because the light had faded, I understood the day had not only been about unplugging. It had been a practice in listening without interruption, and in that listening I found a steadiness I could carry back into the noise.

A day like this will not suit everyone, but even a small pocket of time to sit in silence and notice without agenda can open a clearer channel to yourself. If you cannot hear your own voice beneath the static, it becomes almost impossible to truly hear anyone else's.

The practice of staying

There are still days I forget that doing all the right things does not mean I am fully here. I move through conversations with practiced empathy, bow in and teach with steady breath, respond to messages with care and check in on the people I love, yet beneath it all there is an ache I cannot quite name. It is not loud or urgent, only quietly there, a weight in the chest, a fog behind the eyes, a sense that something is slightly off.

For years I ignored that feeling, or reframed it, or explained it away. I told myself I was just tired, that it had been a long week, that nothing was really wrong. Sometimes that was true. Other times, what I was really saying was, *Please do not ask me to feel this right now.* And beneath that, even deeper, *Please do not leave me alone with it either.*

One afternoon I pulled into the driveway after work and stayed in the car, listening to the soft ticking of the engine as it cooled. Junko and I were still living together then, though the marriage had already begun to thin. You could feel it in the air the way you do when a fire has gone out, with everything still in place yet cold and unmoving. The boys were not home, the house was quiet, and for the first time all day, so was I.

No podcast, no messages, no movement. Just me, alone in the car, letting the silence gather around me. I did not cry or collapse, but something in me began to open, slowly and gently, like a leak I had not noticed until I finally stopped moving. Sadness and tiredness surfaced, followed by something like grief, softer at the edges, and a tenderness I had been bracing against for months.

My hand reached for my phone, ready to call someone, open a tab or fill the space with anything but this. Something in me said, *Don't*, and for once I listened. I closed my eyes and placed a hand on my chest, not to fix anything or steady my breath but simply to feel what was

Listening to Yourself

there. My breath was tight and shallow, yet I stayed with it. No agenda, no performance, only a quiet kind of being.

In that stillness something in me softened. It was not resolution or clarity, but it was enough to feel met, not by someone else but by myself. It came from the part of me I usually override, the part that is not teaching or problem-solving or turning pain into insight, just the human part that aches sometimes and wants only to be held.

I realised I could hold space for myself in the same way I had been learning to hold it for others. I could stay not as a guide or a fixer but as a witness, telling myself I am here, you do not have to explain, you are safe with me. That was new.

It did not fix the marriage or change the day, but it gave me something I had not felt in a long time, a quiet trust in myself. Now, when that familiar weight begins to gather, when the world grows loud and something in me goes still, I return to that moment in the car, not to escape but to come home.

Because sometimes the one who most needs you to stay is not asking for insight, steadiness or strength. They are hoping you will stay with them, and with what is real, until the silence feels like company instead of absence.

Afterword

I called this book *Shut Up – A journey into the lost art of listening* for two reasons.

First, "Shut Up" was never meant for anyone else, it was meant for me. It became my personal shorthand for those moments when I feel the urge to speak and instead choose to stay with what is already here. It is a reminder to unclench, quiet the narrator, stop managing the moment and actually meet it.

And "a journey" felt right because that is exactly what it has been. It is not a destination or a technique I have mastered, but a path I continue to walk, sometimes with clarity and sometimes with a limp, yet always moving forward and always returning.

Sensei once told me, "Do not think you will ever *get* Aikido. There will always be something to learn."

I nodded, believing I understood. But back then I still believed in the promise of arrival. I thought that if I trained hard enough, reflected deeply enough and listened well enough, there would come a moment when I could finally exhale and say, I have it now.

That moment never came, not with Aikido, not with parenting, not with relationships and certainly not with listening. There is always more to learn, and often the learning comes in moments I would rather avoid. It shows up in missed cues, hard conversations and quiet reminders from the people closest to me that I have drifted again.

The people I love could tell you how often I forget, how often I fall back into old patterns and how many moments I still miss even while writing this book, especially while writing this book. I became absorbed, even obsessed. I wanted to get every sentence, every section and every story right. I was trying to offer something honest and useful. Teaching, as Sensei would say, what I still need to learn.

Then one night Antoinette looked at me, gently but unmistakably, and said, "You are spending a lot of time on your book. You are not present with me. I need you here, with me, now." Just like that, I was called back. The irony landed hard. I had been writing about presence, connection, and the sacred act of staying with another person, yet I was not hearing her. Not truly. I was elsewhere, constructing a map of a place I had forgotten to stand in. That moment hurt, but I am glad it did.

Listening is not only about tenderness, it is also about being called back. It is about hearing what you do not want to hear and allowing it to shift your posture, bringing you back to what matters most.

That, I have come to believe, is the real work. Not to get everything right but to return, again and again.

Afterword

I still forget. I still flinch. But I keep coming back, not because I should but because I care, because it matters to me and to the people I love most.

So if you find yourself drifting, offering advice instead of your undivided attention, zoning out when things get uncomfortable or nodding along while your mind is two rooms away, you are not failing, you are simply human. Breathe in and feel the ground beneath your feet. Let yourself return, fully, to what is here.

This is the art, the work and the quiet life of listening.

References

1. Misra, S., Cheng, L., Genevie, J., & Yuan, M. (2016). The iPhone Effect. Environment and Behavior, 48(2), 275-298. https://doi.org/10.1177/0013916514539755

2. Feng, B., & Magen, E. (2015). Relationship closeness predicts unsolicited advice giving in supportive interactions. Journal of Social and Personal Relationships. Advance online publication. https://doi.org/10.1177/0265407515592262

3. Qin, C., Li, Y., Wang, T., Zhao, J., Tong, L., Yang, J., & Liu, Y. (2024). Too much social media? Unveiling the effects of determinants in social media fatigue. Frontiers in Psychology, 15. https://www.frontiersin.org/journals/psychology/articles/10.3389/fpsyg.2024.1277846/full

4. Asker, D. & Dinas, E. (2019). Thinking Fast and Furious: Emotional Intensity and Opinion Polarization in Online Media. Public Opinion Quarterly, 83(3), 487–509. Advance-access manuscript available at Oxford Academic https://academic.oup.com/poq/article-abstract/83/3/487/5566253

5. Bodie, G. D., Vickery, A. J., Cannava, K., & Jones, S. M. (2013). The Relative Effectiveness of Active Listening in Initial Interactions. International Journal of

Listening, 27(2), 102–120. Advance-access manuscript available at Taylor & Francis Online https://www.tandfonline.com/doi/pdf/10.1080/10904018.2013.813234

6. Gunnar, M. R., & Hostinar, C. E. (2015). The social buffering of the hypothalamic–pituitary–adrenocortical (HPA) axis in humans: Developmental and experiential determinants. Social Neuroscience, 10(5), 479–488. https://doi.org/10.1080/17470919.2015.1070747

7. Bangerter, A., Chevalley, E., & Derouwaux, S. (2010). Managing third-party interruptions in conversations: Effects of duration and conversational role. Journal of Language and Social Psychology, 29(2), 235–244. https://doi.org/10.1177/0261927X09359591

8. Farley, S. D., Ashcraft, A. M., Stasson, M. F., & Nusbaum, R. L. (2008). Attaining status at the expense of likeability: Pilfering power through conversational interruption. Journal of Nonverbal Behavior, 32(4), 241–260. https://link.springer.com/article/10.1007/s10919-008-0054-x

9. Fairhurst, M. T., McGlone, F., & Croy, I. (2021). Affective touch: A communication channel for social exchange. Current Opinion in Behavioral Sciences, 43, 54–61. https://doi.org/10.1016/j.cobeha.2021.04.020Eisenberger, N. I., Taylor, S. E., Gable, S. L., Hilmert, C. J., & Lieberman, M. D. (2007). Neural pathways link social support to attenuated neuroendocrine stress responses.

NeuroImage, 35(4), 1601–1612. https://doi.org/10.1016/j.neuroimage.2007.01.038

10. Norcross, J. C., & Lambert, M. J. (2018). Psychotherapy Relationships That Work III: Therapist, clinician, and patient contributions. Psychotherapy, 55(4), 303–315. https://doi.org/10.1037/pst0000193

11. Heinrichs, M., Baumgartner, T., Kirschbaum, C., & Ehlert, U. (2003). Social support and oxytocin interact to suppress cortisol and subjective responses to psychosocial stress. Biological Psychiatry, 54(12), 1389–1398. https://doi.org/10.1016/S0006-3223(03)00465-7

12. Newton, E. L. (1990). Tappers and listeners: The curse of knowledge in communication (Unpublished doctoral dissertation, Stanford University). https://studylib.net/doc/9898118/the-curse-of-knowledge

13. Mobbs, D., Hagan, C. C., Dalgleish, T., Silston, B., & Prévost, C. (2015). The ecology of human fear: Survival optimization and the nervous system. Frontiers in Neuroscience, 9, 55. https://doi.org/10.3389/fnins.2015.00055

14. Brühl, A. B., Baecke, S., & Abler, B. (2013). Mindfulness and emotion regulation—an fMRI study. Social Cognitive and Affective Neuroscience, 9(6), 776–785. https://doi.org/10.1093/scan/nst043

15. Etkin, A., Büchel, C., & Gross, J. J. (2015). The neural bases of emotion regulation. Frontiers in

Neuroscience, 9, 55. https://doi.org/10.3389/fnins.2015.00055

16. Mehrabian, A., & Wiener, M. (1967). Decoding of Inconsistent Communications. Journal of Personality and Social Psychology, 6(1), 109–114.

17. Coan, J. A., Schaefer, H. S., & Davidson, R. J. (2006). Lending a hand: Social regulation of the neural response to threat. Psychological Science, 17(12), 1032–1039. https://doi.org/10.1111/j.1467-9280.2006.01832.x

18. Morrison, I. (2016). Keep Calm and Cuddle On: Social Touch as a Stress Buffer. Adaptive Human Behavior and Physiology, 2, 344–362. https://doi.org/10.1007/s40750-016-0052-x

19. Blau, V. C., Maurer, U., Tottenham, N., & McCandliss, B. D. (2007). The face-specific N170 component is modulated by emotional facial expression. Behavioral and Brain Functions, 3, Article 7. https://behavioralandbrainfunctions.biomedcentral.com/articles/10.1186/1744-9081-3-7

20. Gottman, J. M., & Levenson, R. W. (1992). Marital processes predictive of later dissolution: Behavior, physiology, and health. Journal of Personality and Social Psychology, 63(2), 221–233. https://doi.org/10.1037/0022-3514.63.2.221

21. Weinstein, N., & Itzchakov, G. (in press 2025). Empathic listening satisfies speakers' psychological needs and well-being (Registered Report). Journal of

Experimental Social Psychology, 117: 104716. https://doi.org/10.1016/j.jesp.2024.104716

22. Weinstein, N., & Itzchakov, G. (2025). Empathic listening satisfies speakers' psychological needs and well-being: A registered report. Journal of Experimental Social Psychology, 117, Article 104716. https://doi.org/10.1016/j.jesp.2024.104716

23. Edmondson, A. C. (1999). Psychological safety and learning behavior in work teams. Administrative Science Quarterly, 44(2), 350–383. https://doi.org/10.2307/2666999

24. Rozovsky, J. (2015, November 17). The five keys to a successful Google team. re:Work with Google. Retrieved July 2025, from Google's official re:Work site https://rework.withgoogle.com/en/guides/understanding-team-effectiveness/

Acknowledgement

To my family, friends, colleagues, and Aikido training partners, thank you for the countless ways you have contributed to my life, and in turn, to this book. Your presence, patience, and generosity have shaped my understanding of connection and reminded me, again and again, what it means to truly listen. This work carries pieces of all of you.

About the author

Richard Dillon is a writer, partner, and father who has spent much of his life exploring what it means to listen deeply. After years working in design and web development, he moved into leadership, where he discovered that true influence and trust are built not through what we say, but through how we listen.

He holds a diploma in counselling, which he pursued not to practise professionally but to better understand the psychology of relationships and communication. This study, combined with his personal experiences, continues to shape his writing and his approach to life.

A long-time practitioner of the martial art Aikido, Richard has learned that discernment, humility, and steady presence matter as much off the mat as they do within training. These lessons are woven throughout his work, alongside reflections from family life and personal growth.

Richard lives in Melbourne with his partner Antoinette and his two sons. Shut Up – A journey into the lost art of listening is his first book.